ANATOM
OF EVIL

Fra Angelico (1387–1455), *THE BLESSED AND THE CONDEMNED*

ANATOMY OF EVIL

RUTH NANDA ANSHEN

MOYER BELL LIMITED
MT. KISCO, NEW YORK

Photography: Nathan Rabin
Cover Design: Marcus Ratliff

Library of Congress Cataloging in Publication Data

Anshen, Ruth Nanda.
  Anatomy of Evil.
  Reprint: Originally published: The Reality of the Devil.
New York : Harper & Row, 1972. With new Prologue.
  Includes new index.
  1. Devil. 2. Good and evil. I. Anshen, Ruth Nanda.
Reality of the devil. II. Title.
[BT981.A57 1985]   235'.4   85-19505
ISBN 0-918825-15-6 (pbk.)

Pablo Picasso (1881-1973), *THE CHARNEL HOUSE* © The Museum of
Modern Art, New York

Duccio di Buoninsegna (ca. 1278-1319), *TEMPTATION OF CHRIST ON
THE MOUNTAIN* © The Frick Collection, New York

Moyer Bell Limited would like to extend special thanks to the staffs of
The Frick Collection and The New York Public Library for their help in
the picture research.

Printed in the United States of America

During their dialogue, the Devil speaks to Ivan:

"No, you are not someone apart, you are myself. You are I and nothing more...."

Ivan replies:

"You are the incarnation of myself, but only of one side of me... of my thoughts and feelings, but only the nastiest and stupidest of them.... You are myself—with a different face. You just say what I am thinking, you are incapable of saying anything new!"

Dostoevski, *The Brothers Karamazov, Part IV,*
Chapter IX

Ὦ πόποι, οἷον δή νυ δεονς βροτοὶ αἰτιοωνται. Ἐξ ἡμεων γάρ φασι κάκ ἔμμεναι οἱ δὲ καὶ αὐτοὶ σφῆσιν ἀτασφαλίῃσιν ὑπερ μόρον ἄλγε ἔχουσιν.

"O alas, how now do men accuse the gods! For they say evils come from us. But they themselves, by (reason) of their sins, have sufferings beyond those destined (for) them."

Homer, *Odyssey* I. 32-34

"God allowed evil to exist, woven into the texture of the world, in order to increase man's freedom and his will to prove his moral strength in overcoming it."

From The Philosophy of Gnosticism

CONTENTS

Illustrations precede each chapter

ACKNOWLEDGMENTS

I wish to express my warm appreciation to Professor Meyer Shapiro, Mr. A. Hyatt Mayor, Professor Adolph Lowe, and Professor Morton Smith for their generous suggestions in the preparation of this manuscript.

Ruth Nanda Anshen

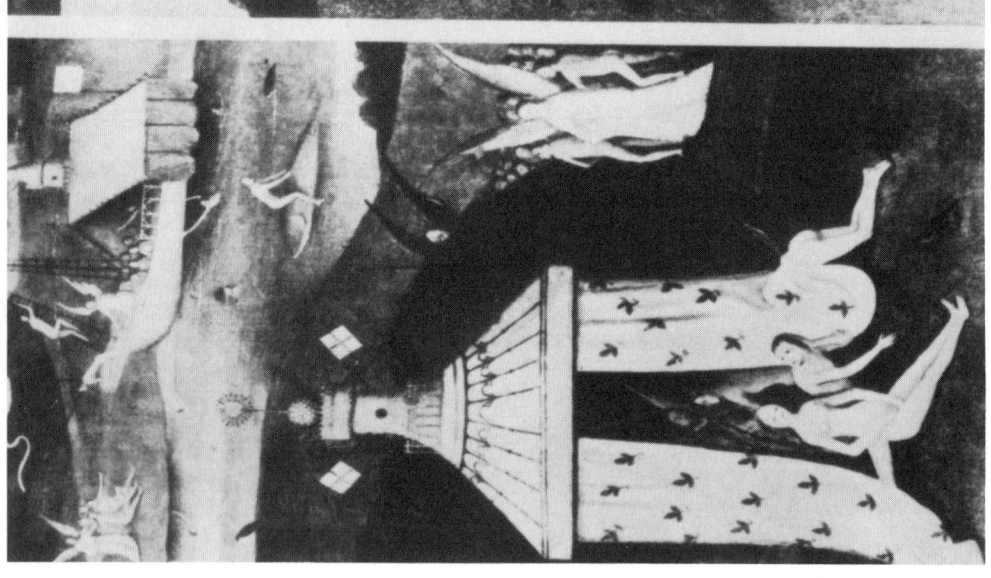

Hieronymous Bosch (ca. 1450-1516), *PARADISE AND HELL*

PREFACE

THE CITY OF GOD AND THE CITY OF SATAN

In the Western world we have all been taught that truth and error, good and evil, God and the Devil cannot be put on the same level and enjoy the same freedom. And yet the experience of both man and history proves the contrary.

In this book I try to tell the story of man and woman, of that part of them which points to their deep need to choose—too often, alas—the Evil rather than the Good. Here the theme is directed toward their sinfulness, distortions of reality, degradation, the tendency to drift toward the subhuman even while they may aspire to redemption and salvation and shed the tragic tears of Heraclitus or sucumb to the demonic laughter of Democritus.

Although I am attempting to deal with the reality of the Devil, this is only another way of saying that the Devil is in us—we who take leave of our senses and fall prey to our own passions, to vice, selfishness, falsehood, vanity, lust, greed, superstition, fanaticism. The biblical question of why man and woman may know the Good but choose the Evil has never been answered satisfactorily in spite of many exegetical explanations. Perhaps there is no answer except in the paradox of the ambiguity of all life.

As a child, I was deeply impressed with the juxtaposition of Good and Evil. Then, as I grew older, more educated, more questioning, I began to wonder if I were wrong. Perhaps my knowledge was insufficient, or somewhere there was an error in my thinking or in the interpretation of my own experience. But I clung to what appeared to me to be an unalterable truth: that Good and Evil, God and the Devil, are equal in power, though of course not identical in substance (in spite of the obvious paradox of this position). And this, history has proved again and again.

That Evil is an inherent element in the universe I soon saw all around me: in the pitiless affliction of suffering on the innocent, the helpless, the just; in the relentless eruptions and devastations of nature against human life. Above all, I saw the unbearable indifference of the universe to human aspirations and human suffering. As Euripides said: "This is a universe where justice is accidental and innocence no protection."

That the universe is not conscious of itself, and a human being is (and therefore has freedom and will), does indeed make a difference. However, there lurks in me the conviction that somehow there exists an ineradicable equality of Good and Evil in nature as in both women and men: beauty and ugliness, health and disease, creation and destruction, peace and anguish. This conclusion, heretical though it may seem, is the fruit of years of my experience and reflection.

Our inner world is deeply disturbing. We wrestle endlessly with the problems of freedom and our own ultimate destiny and meaning. We sway between the beautiful and the monstrous, and we make the monstrous look true. We are obsessed with the desire to condemn this slavery in its manifold aspects (whether psychological, technological or political), to resist the rationalistic civilization engulfing us and smothering our deepest desires in a mass of duties, submissions and inhibitions, until we finally protest from the innermost depths of our being by negation, rebellion, and psychosis, which culminate in our ultimate denunciation of self and society.

This protest is also part of the natural law of life. And so we have what has become the crisis of our modern civilization: the unleashing of two irreconcilable forces, reason and revolution. On the one hand, there is the rationalizing of the human being and of society, a rationalism that makes a person more bestial than the beast; and on the other hand, there is our personal struggle for freedom and reason. The individual person alone has the conscious capacity to bear suffering. This capacity is *the* characteristic of human nature, and demonstrates the highest form of life in the manifestation of freedom.

"Homo sum nil humani a me alienum puto," the great humanist, Pico della Mirandola* said in the 15th century. This sums up our present human predicament, as it has for past ages. The grandeur and misery, the serenity and aberrations—all things are possible for us. And yet it is not in spite of the reality of Evil, or in spite of the Devil's immortality, but rather, because of them that we must finally come to terms with the way things are. Something new has been born in the consciousness of Western thought and we begin to recognize our formidable adversary in history and in ourselves as an inevitable, though sometimes obscured, aspect of the Good. For it was God who created all things, including Satan (Evil), and God allowed a vestige of the Good to reside within the fallen Angel as a punishment (and endless torture) for this act of apostasy from heaven, from God.

And now we are brought down to the level of a lost child. This indifference of nature, or to be blasphemous, this badly messed-up creation—this is what confronts us. Thus we are compelled to ask: What are the sources of our criteria for our choices, our values, since some of those of past history are no longer valid? We have eaten of a new tree of knowledge and the trend is irreversible.

---

*Quoted from "Heauton Timorovmenos", Act I, Sc. I, line 25; by Publius Torence (190–159 B.C.).

No longer can we gloss over the primacy of suffering in life. No longer can we say, "Admiro quia absurdum," on which professional philosophers and theologians over the past centuries have spent their lives. When Job says to the Lord, "Why don't you pay attention to me?" and the Lord replies, "Who are you that I should pay attention to you?" Job answers, "Even though Thou crusheth me, yet will I defy Thee." This must be our answer. True, life is exactly as the Lord says it is. Nevertheless, the Promethean protest must never be silenced by human lame submission. And even though we can do nothing about this, we need not for that reason say Yes to it.

I have tried to deal with Evil phenomenologically; and with the Devil as a personality that appears in the Western world. This necessitated the neglect of demons, witches, sorcerers and their apprentices as they manifest themselves in the cosmogony of the East and in ancient and primitive cultures.

The figure of the Devil has dominated the imagination of the West for fifteen hundred years. History itself is so enormous and complex, the manifestations of the Devil are so numerous, that all I can do here is give some of the outstanding examples among the many diabolical expressions of the Devil's existence, since this personification has an infinite variety, is chameleonlike in nature, and never cloys the appetites it feeds.

We all experience the tragic elements in the transition from our essence to our existence, although the two are never separated into two unrelated systems of the universe or of the individual. At best they constitute a nondual duality. This is a compelling fact of our finiteness; and of our consciousness that we must die: both in what we are and what we do. This is the price we pay for primordial sin as it appears in the story of the fall and as told in the book of Genesis. It is an event that happened, as a mythological symbol, long, long ago in a special place, and it happened to two people, Eve and then Adam.

God appeared as an individual person in space and time and laid claim to universal validity in the Western world. The serpent became the symbol of the demonic elements in human nature which tend to Evil. Then followed the magical nature of the two trees: the Tree of Knowledge and the Tree of Life, the birth of sexual consciousness and the curse on Adam and Eve and on their progeny.

The eating of the Tree of Knowledge while excluding the Tree of Life has led to the eventual emphasis on progress, on history, and on the concept and responsibility of the person—all previously lacking in Eastern theories of the universe and of the individual. The idea of progress assured Western thought, erroneously, of the inevitable victory of the Good as a positive force in history and in human life, while Evil was considered to be a negative principle eventually to be overcome by God's grace, by a fortunate fate, by self-discipline, a righteous life, and now even by technology itself. Divine Providence, synonymous with progress, triumphs for both Hegel and Marx. For Hegel, it is triumphant in his own epoch, while for Marx progress will triumph ultimately in some vague, indefinite utopian future. But the optimism inherent in the idea of progress in the nineteenth century led inevitably to the negation of progress historically, morally, and spiritually, in the twentieth century. Marx himself emphasizes the dehumanization in the historical existence of the individual as a refutation of personal faith in an automatic, inevitable progress and eventual harmony between individuals, the individual and nature, the individual and God.

Each of us passionately yearns for some belief in a personal fulfillment. The horrible catastrophes in recent history, however, have completely destroyed the belief in the existence of a rational Providence. Just as faith was shattered and overshadowed in the ancient world, faith in a redeemed world of the West also has been annihilated. The evolutionary emphasis on the idea of progress, on the self-related, self-preserving, and self-continuing aspects of life, has been obliterated. Evolution and devolution are inseparable, are in fact equal, though not identical. And it is the consciousness of the reality of the presence of both in all human experience, in all nature, that this book attempts to develop. Evil, even as Good, is a positive, dynamic reality. This is a truth profoundly misconceived by the prophets of the ultimate triumph of Good over Evil, as we learn from Spencer, Darwin, and even William James, who (no less than we ourselves) were incapable of accepting abysmal atrocities and diabolic achievements, even when a Hitler, for example, stated in no ambiguous terms what his program of annihilation would be. History is irrefutable in this.

Evil, Satan, never will be obliterated so long as human nature remains what it is; so long as potentiality and actuality coexist; so long as the organic is essentially present in the inorganic. For this is reality—not rationalism, which is a distortion of reality as well as of reason. The myths of the Golden Age and the Fall, by which human life and human society were created perfect and free from all Evil, are now destroyed and degraded, and Evil is an essential constituent of human nature, never to be eradicated, even by redemption. But suffering, strength, and even the acceptance of the experience of death can allow us to triumph with dignity and self-esteem, and to transmute tragedy into spiritual and moral transcendence.

Yet, I ask, is this the original destiny of humankind? The baffling question why we are subject to death and Evil remains unanswered. Even philosophy, as we see in the metaphysical speculations of Plato, teaches us that the essential human reaction against the limitations of the physical and intellectual nature of ourselves will exist forever.

But, according to the doctrine of redemption dominating Christian theology we are indeed slaves of Satan. Not even the tragic conflict between the forces of darkness and the forces of light, culminating in the crucifixion of the Son of God and His resurrection, could triumph over Satan. Thus Christianity, in spite of its implacable monotheism and myth of redemption, has failed to achieve the ultimate and logical conclusion of universal salvation, the final and total elimination of Evil on which the West pinned its faith. For with its doctrine of the everlastingness of hell, Christianity assigned an eternal existence to Evil and suffering.

I have always been profoundly impressed with the ancient mythic difference between Christianity and Zoroastrianism. The latter bestowed on Evil an eternal origin but refused to it an eternal existence in the future, allowing it to culminate in an effulgence of unending light; while Christianity reversed the human condition, denying to Evil an eternal source but granting to it an iron, unalterable immortality.

For myself, I conclude that freedom and will coexist with determinism and predestination; total depravity with the infinite obligation to do good; irresistible divine grace with the finite human capacity of resisting it and spurning it; freedom of choice with fatalism. All this may lead to salvation for the very, very few; but for most of us, in one tragic way or another, there remains the fate of falling into the clutches of a tormented but still triumphant Devil.

The ultimate evil is far more profound than any specific evil, since it possesses an ontological character, lying in the very nature of nature and the nature of the individual. Everything entails loss. And it is the nature

of evil that the character of things become mutually
obstructive. Freedom and choice, therefore, consist si-
multaneously in the measuring of evil and the process of
its evasion.* The depths of life demand choice which can
result in the elimination of some obstruction to the
good. "In our cosmological construction we are, therefore, left with the final opposites; joy and sorrow, good
and evil, disjunction and conjunction—that is to say, the
many in the one—flux and permanence, greatness and
triviality, freedom and necessity, God and the World."† It
is the thesis of this book that although there is a
possible dualism implied in Whitehead, it is not at all a
true dualism, since he always warns us that we may not
"bifurcate the universe into two systems of reality."
Thus, we could in fact conclude that, even in Whitehead,
good and evil though equal in power are not identical in
substance, since we possess freedom and choice.

What, then, remains? What may still render life mean-
ingful and dignified in spite of some problematical eschatological future which may be blessed or damned but
which in all probability will continue to be both?

Perhaps for the fleeting moment that each person's life
fills, we may rise above time and an indifferent eternity
and transcend the diabolic forces which infuse both
nature and us. We then may experience that ray of light
which pierces the darkness. For the forces of Good
desperately need our support against the forces of Evil,
and above all against that which is worse than Evil:
satanic indifference, a void which monotheistic religions
try to conceal.

For, although the law of entropy and the second law of
thermodynamics, the law of destruction, is an inevitable
reality of our experience as individuals in nature, there

---

*Cf. Alfred North Whitehead, *Process and Reality* (New York: The
Macmillan Company, 1929).
  †Ibid.

is, at the same time, an anti-entropic force, an energy which affirms its dependence on our creative powers. This is not at all a form of Manichaeism, of the dualistic battle between the powers of Good and Evil. On the contrary, it is rather the basic unity of all life in which there are no antinomies. And this unity belongs to the realm of values, values which cannot be rejected any more than a painting can be separated from its canvas and pigment. And it is no difficult task to show that those who scorn such values in the name of technology, scientific method of political duplicities, of racial prejudices, or of economic necessity are themselves actuated to this scorn by dogmas, ideologies, or other value-impregnated thought-forms only in the arena of the human relevance of what they do.

Ruth Nanda Anshen

THE TWO PRINCIPALS, Ancient Africa, Upper Niger

PROLOGUE

Throughout the text to follow the masculine pronoun has been used to refer to both God and Satan. If I were writing in the Persian or Turkish languages there would be no distinction between the masculine and feminine pronouns since in those languages the pronouns are androgynous, without gender. In most other languages, however, we are confronted with a problem concerning which the existential phenomenon of contemporary history demands our attention.

Concerning women we can no longer invoke intellectual inequality in comparison with the creative powers in men. We can no longer compare Hypatia with Plato. Woman is emerging as a political, economic, historical, cultural inevitability, in spite of the tradition that woman's role was only to inspire and to nourish. We must remember that the Muses were feminine. Also it was not God the Father but the Goddess Thiamat, herself created out of primordial matter, who created all life. We now must accept the reality that men and women are equal yet different. We must also remember that woman creates the creator, and in the past was the center of the family, creating a second womb for the children. Woman now has become both instrument and ornament.

Before 835 A.D. of the Christian era, among the Church Fathers, woman was considered to be merely a

charming animal. She had no soul and was incapable of
sin, an honorable condition not without its advantages. It
was the Council of Agde, after rigorous dispute, that
official dignity was bestowed upon woman endowing her
with the same creative powers possessed by men.

Life moves toward unity. The axis of world history
passes through the fifth century B.C. in the midst of the
spiritual process between 800 and 200 B.C.–Confucius
and Lao-tse in China, the Upanishads and Buddha in
India, Zarathustra in Persia, the prophets, in Palestine,
Homer and the philosophers in Greece. Although it may
appear that those creative minds had nothing in common, they became the origins of the great historical
world-civilizations and that those origins, in their very
differentiations, had something uniquely in common. We
also see at once that woman *explicitly* does not appear.
That was a time when mythologies were being discarded
or used for the foundations of the great world religions
with their concept of One Transcendent God. Philosophy
makes its appearance everywhere; being is discovered as
a whole differentiating human beings from other forms
of life and for the first time man becomes conscious of
consciousness. All fundamental categories of thinking,
all basic tenets of beliefs were created during that
period. The world history of humanity derives its structure from that time.

And now toward the end of the twentieth century we
find ourselves, in our evolved consciousness, at the
beginning of the historical unity of the human species.
There is now a new axis, the incarnation of an ideal axis
around which humanity in its movement is drawn together.

At the same time, however, we are confronted with the
powers of evil in history. The immensity of moral and
physical evil in the world and the overwhelming manifestation of the demonic and its tragic consequences in

history have always been an existential as well as theoretical argument against the acceptance of any belief in historical providence. No future justice and happiness can annihilate the injustice and suffering of the past. The progressive-utopian assumptions contradict the elements of freedom for good and evil with which each person is born. Where the power for good increases, the power for evil increases also.

And just as neither God nor the Devil possesses gender so evil is also genderless. Thus, the attribute of sexuality is irrelevant and the pronoun "he" applied to God or Satan is simply the linguistic device employed in Western cosmogony.

However, when we consider the human person–sex–gender–we confront a vastly different situation. Women experience reality in a somewhat different manner from the experience men have. Women create the creator. Women create the second womb for the children in the home. For women, motherhood sanctifies life. Yes, life is sacred. Men participate as an instrument. Women are the Gaea principle of creation; men, the Antaeus. Thus women love differently. There is such pity in it. And it is all the more piteous because even beneath its distracted doubts and fears, justified or unjustified, there is the deep ocean of love, the triumph of a deeper passionate love over physical passion and the splendid affirmation of the spiritual supremacy of love. For love is nourished by a mysterious unity: a non-dual duality. And *eros* is rescued by *agape*, for *agape* is incapable of destruction, does not even wish to destroy what destroys. Yet it is possible for women and men to experience fidelity which secures itself against unfaithfulness by becoming accustomed not to separate love from desire. For if desire moves swiftly and promiscuously, love is slow and difficult. Love is a pledge and exacts nothing less than this pledge in order to disclose its true nature. Thus though women and men are equal, they are different. But then, Aha ! the Devil enters.... One prays, "Our Father who art in Heaven, Hallowed be Thy Name... Deliver us from evil...." And there's the rub. The uniting of that which is separated is threatened. Nicholas of Cusa spoke of the nearness and distance of women and men as "coincidence of opposites." Love then is the dynamic union of that which was separated.

Nevertheless, we now are face-to-face with the demand for social equality among all strata of human beings including women and children. There is a worldwide effort to conquer mass poverty; the release of nuclear energy and the push into outer space; also the development of cybernetics and the breaking of the genetic code; the challenging achievements of biomedical research and the insights into the unconscious mind including its symbolic expressions in art, music and literature. Above all, there is the awareness that the individual is a particle, among other particles, in a breathing universe, part of the unfolding, living, dynamic process of the manifold rhythms of evolutionary life. Boundaries have vanished. For the atom in a star is the same as the atom in the human organism.

We ask whether science can provide us with any clear ideas, independently of metaphysical principles. Science is based on the concept of law, the law of nature. The idea is that there are many things in the world whose behavior toward each other always exemplifies fixed rules. These rules evidently indicate recurrences that never fail. Nevertheless, we are perplexed by the connection of the laws to behaving things. Obviously, behavior differs among different peoples, cultures, areas. In addition, behavior differs widely on the moon, the sun, in the interior of a dense star, in interstellar space. Yet the molecules in the laws of chemistry are the same everywhere. They express the mutual behavior of molecules, packed with sufficient closeness. The chemical laws are relevant to the interrelations of molecules. In empty space we are driven back to the fundamental electromagnetic laws controlling the flux of Energy as an immutable principle. Alfred North Whitehead has stated in his *The Principle of Relativity*:

>...that the molecular theory, the wave theory of light, and finally the electro-magnetic theory of things in general have, as it seems, set up for scientific investigation a society of entities such as ether, molecules, and electrons, which are intrinsically incapable of direct observation. When Sir Ernest Rutherford at Cambridge University knocks a molecule to pieces, he does not see a molecule or an electron. What he observes is a flash of light (but he knows that molecules exist closely packed together).... If we are to avoid an unfortunate bifurcation (of the Universe into two systems of reality) we must construe our knowledge of the apparent world as being an individual experience of something which is more than personal. Nature is thus a totality including individual experiences so that we must reject the distinction between nature as it really is and the experience of it which are purely psychological. Our experiences of the apparent world are nature itself.

Thus it includes the presence of electrons and photons. And these photons when placed parallel to each other actually, if indeed metaphorically, "speak" together. They communicate. In fact, in relation to the evolution and complexity of consciousness and experience, we may say with impunity as well as with reverence that the principle of Energy is synonymous with the immutable divine substance, with what is called God, as well as with the diabolical substance known as Satan.

Anatomy of Evil is an attempt to expose the reality of

the relevance of God and Satan in history, since they are synonymous, indivisible. We are not dealing with the universe of Newton, but with one that is faithful to the laws of Einstein in which matter and energy are interchangeable and indivisible. From this we must deduce that there is an intimate interrelationship between the world of the mind and the world of matter, the world of the good and the world of evil, since it is with the Energy of our consciousness that we think and make observations. In other words we cannot separate ourselves from the events that we are observing, often even actually determining what takes place. We now may use the word Energy, an immutable principle of the universe both abstract and concrete as are also God and the Devil. And although it is a risk to follow the still, small voice of conscience, it is a greater risk not to. Thus, choice in action is decisive, and in choice our destiny dwells.

INTRODUCTION

It is by no means certain that the Devil exists. Such uncertainty, however, cannot comfort the pious; for it is uncertainty that makes hell of our life. Nor should the skeptic and the rationalist smile disdainfully; for the existence of the Devil explains the amount of evil and misery, of hypocrisy and falsehood, which fills the world.

But whether or not the Devil exists, he certainly is not fashionable. Even the church seems to have eliminated him from its lexicon. Now when the Church rallies all her forces in the crusade for God and the Good against the powers of Evil, the great adversary himself is not named. We may wonder whether this strange silence—perhaps a politic concession to the scientific age—does not deprive the crusade of much of its blood and vigor. Or does the church recoil from focusing upon the Devil and his abject glory and power, well aware that splendor and might, once they surpass the human standard, paralyze man and render him a willful follower and helpless victim of Evil?

It was Cardinal Newman who said that glowing and passionate faith was no longer the privilege and mark of his times and that all that could be expected and desired of the believer was to be resistant to doubt. Since Newman wrote these words, the power of faith has deteriorated. The disintegration of religious and social tradition, the revolution of the scientific world-picture and, more trenchant than anything, the undermining of authority in every sphere of life have eaten away the very foundations of the power and will to believe. Worse than skepticism and militant atheism is indifference. Skepticism still holds its object in sight and within reach. Militant atheism challenges and thereby strengthens the defensive forces of faith, and more often than not hides the need and will to believe. Indifference, however, is the archenemy of faith. Thus indifference is the pasture of the Devil.

If this deduction is valid, the Devil must be the lord of our time. The Supreme Being does not condescend to change His aspect; it is the Devil who delights in assuming various disguises to lure his prey, to convince man that he does not exist, as Baudelaire warned. But in times of indifference no disguises are necessary. Indifference engenders confusion, and in confusion values are drowned, decisions are suspected as capricious or opportunistic; the constant anxiety over the present moment undermines existence and essence.

Nothing could be more welcome to the Devil. He is the master of the moment. He grants the instantaneous gratification of every wish and whim and, in doing so, dissolves life into an uninterrupted succession of inchoate desires and their fulfillment—the great horoscope of our time.

The Devil is so cunning he may use our own certainty and self-satisfaction to catch us with his snares. While we congratulate ourselves for having found the matrix of our present existence, he may sneak into our souls and lead us astray. It is not that what has been said must be revoked, nor even changed. But assuming that we are dealing with a power of extreme and fiendish subtlety, the possibility cannot be excluded that we may have played into the Devil's hand without knowing it. If so, the picture of our present world situation, while remain ing factually untouched, requires another interpretation and evaluation.

Let us then base our reasoning on the hypothesis that the Devil's ascendancy in our time is less violent than we have assumed it to be. There is no denying the fact that Western evolution has permitted indifference and confusion to spread in the spiritual realm. To many, such an idea is abhorrent and monstrous; indifference, confusion, and despair are not the spontaneous outcome of our own nature and will. They represent diabolical insinuations and whisperings and must be considered the feelers, the antennae, that Evil sends out as its vanguards to sound the terrain. If this interpretation were accepted, it clearly would mean that the Devil is only knocking at the door—very audibly, it is true—but that the moment may still be far off, if it arrives at all, when he will make his entry with all his paraphernalia. It is a theological problem, and of no concern here, whether or not this second view seems more consoling than the first and which of the two is more likely to exonerate us from guilt.

Even from this summary analysis of an actual and concrete situation we may get a foretaste of the intricate and forbidding riddles and the controversial issues which inevitably must be confronted once the Devil is recognized in human affairs. We feel how the ground under our feet begins to tremble and give way. Everything loses its identity and unmistakable meaning, and we see that our opinions and planning must depend more upon will and decision than upon knowledge and insight, and that we trust our fate to an *ignis fatuus* if we rely only upon our intellect. Indeed, how could it be otherwise? The Devil feeds on confusion, but he himself is not confused. He has his own order and laws, and the disorder he welcomes and, if need be, himself creates is but a movement in his great scheme.

R.N.A.

Felicien Rops (1833-1893), *THE DEVIL SOWING SEEDS OF DISCORD IN THE HAUNTS OF MEN*

I

ON THE DEVIL, OR THAT WHICH DOES NOT EXIST?

The title of this chapter is misleading. It contains the inadequate and in fact untranslatable translation of the title that pre-Socratic philosophers gave to the books in which they expounded their ideas on nature as opposed to those constituting their main works, which were dedicated to the philosophy of the essence of things. The implication was that there could not be a true knowledge of nature as the world of phenomena because such knowledge had to start from and be based on the data of sense perception, which are inevitably uncertain, deceptive, and transient. On the contrary, so they taught, we possess in pure reason (*logos*) an instrument capable of disclosing reality, absolute truth.

To express the fundamental difference of the two forms of knowledge and their objects, the philosophers used a particle—probably unique among the world's languages—which carries the meaning of a conditioned negation. Thus existential nature—in contradistinction to that which really *is*, the essence, or the true being, the *on*—is that which is, in a certain sense, and under certain conditions, the *ma on*—the nonbeing, *is not*—if measured by absolute standards. With this fundamental restriction, the pre-Socratics sanctioned and themselves promoted science without being lured into looking at science as the supreme, let alone the only, source of knowledge. In this way existential nature became strangely suspended between reality and unreality, being and nonbeing. There is no need to press the comparison.

It appears, however, that the Devil is to all intents and purposes sufficiently real if he shares with nature its conditioned kind and degree of reality—leaving aside and undecided the question as to whether his own conviction or ambition might not induce him heartily to disagree with our definition. Such disagreement would be comprehensible enough since the Devil's form and degree of reality derive from and depend upon the absolute reality, namely, God. As in Greek philosophy, what there is of reality in nature points back to the pure essence revealed by the *logos*. God, indeed, is the point of reference in relation to which the Devil alone exists and from which he has received what there is in him of reality.

Here, however, the strict analogy between nature and the Devil comes to an end. Nature as the totality of actual and potential experience, even if it is represented as a living organism or the universal soul, accepts the superiority of the *logos*, the Absolute. The Devil does not. He is a person and he does what is in his power to emphasize and to insist upon and, beyond that, to take his stand as an independent personality. He refuses to recognize that he is God's creature; he wants and pretends to exist in his own right. And so he starts his unending rebellion.

Is this mythology? Mythology, we know, reaches into realms and depths from which the concept is barred or to which the concept can only lead the way. So if the Devil is the product of mythology, it is a mythology with which we are all familiar because it constitutes a part of ourselves. The father-image and its meaning and implications are well known. It could well be that behind the father and, to speak in Freudian terms, the leader of the primitive horde, there rises a greater figure of greater momentum. Let us then suggest and maintain that the psychoanalytical interpretation does not exhaust the "father-complex" if only because psychoanalytical theory, despite the wide scope of its applications, is and remains a medical therapy in origin. Psychoanalysis— and Freud was the first to concede it—is conditioned by the time into which it was born and by its therapeutic aim. It is not an end but a road and a method.

So the father-complex may hide a mystery of another order and of a more appalling nature, the rebellion of man against being a creature, that is, the rebellion against being created by another, of which parental birth is but one form. Of this rebellion, the Devil is the originator; and though he sprang into existence by a free act of God, he left the spirit of revolt to mankind, in whose beginnings and fate he so effectively interfered in the Garden of Eden. From then on, man revolted against the fact that he owed his life to others, and a hereditary instinct pushed him in vain protest to undo a fact which offended his pride and desire for independence.

The explanation, according to Anastasias and other early Christian writers, of Lucifer's Fall and damnation (which is adopted also by occult doctrines) is lacking in grandeur and psychological probability. The Archangel's refusal to worship Adam in fulfillment of God's command is understandable enough. Who could have worshiped this most miserable of all creatures? And why should God want to test the obedience of the angels, as the legend says? And if God felt really so uncertain about their submissiveness, was there no other than this most absurd test? Or did God value blind obedience beyond anything? If He did, He was quickly and radically refuted. For no sooner had Lucifer refused to pay his respect to Adam than he appeared as the serpent in

Paradise and seduced Eve and Adam to disobey God. These then, obviously, were times when God was still the God of the Old Testament who required obedience not sacrifices. The God of Love, so we might be tempted to argue, could have been expected to have shown compassion for His fallen angel, whom He had hurled for eternal damnation into the pit of hell. The God of Love even could have pitied the progeny of Adam. In fact this story is but rational invention, a legend composed for edifying man and for pedagogical purposes.

The myth, on the contrary, contains a formidable and fundamental truth: the Promethean-like rebellion of the creature against the indelible fact that he is a created being and is constantly reminded of this derivative nature. The Archangel's rebellion may seem utterly devoid of sense. It may seem paradoxical and from the beginning condemned to frustration. Yet in this rebellion Lucifer feels that he *is*, unconditionally *is*. In that moment of revolt he could rejoice—and rightly so—in the consciousness that he was no longer a nonbeing, that he no longer existed merely in relation to God. For not even God could have prevented him from rising in rebellion nor forbidden this experience bought at so high a price, the experience of living an instant of unconditioned existence and freedom. In that moment Lucifer truly transcended himself, rose to equality with God, and for a time-unit that equaled zero and was equivalent with eternity, he sat at the side of God. But how could he not have been aware that God might reduce him to nothing since He had created him out of nothing! Indeed why did not God destroy him? Did God not dare to annihilate the Archangel who, among the celestial hosts, had been nearest to Him? Did He set Lucifer's fate as a deterrent to angels and men? There is no answer. But the fact that God did not destroy him must be an eternal satisfaction to Lucifer. God did not touch him. What did God really do? He banished him from His sight. But the transformation from a power of Good into a power of Evil was Lucifer's own decision.

There, then, sits Lucifer, enthroned in his absolute loneliness. Perhaps his boundless pride did not permit him to anticpate that the fate of rebellion by the created against the creator must inevitably be total isolation—even if there is no damnation. Or it may well be that damnation is nothing but absolute loneliness.

And this price of utter, absolute, implacable loneliness is revealed in the two illustrations in this book: one, in *The Rape of Helen*; and the other, in *Yama, The Death-Devil*, both demonstrating that death and damnation which may be considered synonyms for absolute, unrelated loneliness, is the price man must pay, as Exodus 22:19 teaches. This alienation and despair are the miserable companions of the condition of loneliness and the perversion of nature, in the ultimate inversion of Good into Evil.

It is, of course, a nursery tale that Lucifer is in hell. The story must be read the other way. Wherever Lucifer is, there is hell. And since Lucifer is—potentially—everywhere, so is hell. Lucifer's fate was isolation, and so is the fate of man, who has surrendered to Lucifer and made him his God. He too is absolutely lonely. But while Lucifer can persevere in his isolation, man cannot. Better the communion with Evil then with no one. We do not know the kind of communion the evildoer has with Lucifer himself, but we cannot imagine it to be quite peaceful and wholly satisfactory. Nor can the relation of the evildoer with his equals rescue him from isolation, for it consists in an alliance for the achievement of common, disastrous aims rather than the union of those for whom a positive communion constitutes a primary value.

In Lucifer the humiliating consciousness of being created crushed the feeling of gratitude to God, to whom he owed his existence and his need of nearness to God; and for his rebellion he had to pay a ghastly price. But nothing could denigrate the glory of the moment when, in unimpaired freedom and sovereignty, he rose to be the equal of his Creator. And the obstinate endurance which leads him to persist in contending with God against all odds has its internal greatness. So Lucifer is at the same time a terrible, a triumphant, and a tragic figure. It may not be superfluous to point to the danger which necessarily accompanies a serious effort to arrive at a compassionate understanding of Lucifer's figure and fate—a danger infinitely more intricate than that contained in his multiple snares. But the last word about Lucifer remains still to be said.

William Blake (1757-1827), *SATAN EXULTING OVER EVE*

II

THE ORIGIN AND NATURE
OF EVIL

The biography of Lucifer and the origin of Evil are both centered on God's highly ambiguous and questionable command to worship the poorest of His creations. It is a simple enough story. But as was suggested in the preceding chapter, more can and must be read into the story. Indeed, few myths compare with this one in its inexhaustible significance. The view here adopted is certainly unorthodox in all major points, but its far-reaching consequences are no less contained in the myth than are the traditional interpretations. So we may well continue to take it as a clue for further enlightenment.

We can easily dismiss the argument that the test was entirely useless, since God knew beforehand the reaction of all His angelic creatures. The point was to have them make their decisions and to demonstrate to themselves their own dispositions. More serious, however, is the problem of reconciling divine foresight with freedom of the will. But even this difficulty lies beyond our interest. We might argue that the test was of a nature to unduly humiliate the spiritual substance of angels. We might maintain, with all due reverence, that it was blasphemous—certainly a debasement of the status of a creature, which could not be experienced except as a disproof of God's own word and work. Even if this reasoning is unacceptable, the strongest argument still remains. It belongs, in fact, to another, a moral, order. The test established a scale of moral values that not only recognized blind humility and submissiveness to the will of God as the supreme value but also certified as the valid and decisive proof of the required moral attitude the act of worship. This seems to be a highly questionable procedure, and one that cannot be entirely put aside if Lucifer's action is to be judged.

Such then is our foremost and trenchant problem: Did Lucifer bring Evil into the world? If so, how did his rebellion engender Evil? In what way does this origin reflect upon the nature of Evil?

Case and verdict are equally evident. What crime can be more heinous than the transgression of God's unmistakable command? And can any punishment less than eternal damnation be adequate to the enormity of the crime? Indeed, what else could be the cause or content of Evil if not the rebellion against God and His clearly indicated will? And what else could be the meaning of Lucifer's rebellion?

Here the Devil's advocate comes forward and charges that the accusation itself is wholly erroneous from the psychological as well as from the juridical point of view. He bases his argument on the fact that Lucifer did not rebel against God, but revolted against being a creature or, for that matter, against the status of creature in general. His client, he insists, recognized that the situation planned by God to test His creatures had thrown into clear relief their questionable and untenable status. Only courageous and self-denying action, a kind of civil disobedience, might urge the Almighty to find a solution to a grotesquely defective situation. The advocate insists that the test was a mere farce designed to ridicule the dignity of the angels. Lucifer, indeed, was the only one to penetrate the true significance of the test and to recognize its full weight, or he was at least the only one who dared to give expression and consequence to his insight. It must be supposed—this is not the advocate's least point—that many of the angels who submitted to the test shared Lucifer's attitude but did not have the courage to act according to their conviction. Lucifer by no means ignored the magnificence of the angel's station, but he could not but see the cloven hoof—that is, the ever impending danger threatening the created being. If it is sublime to be a God-creating being, it is at the same time hazardous and terrible. It even might be said that in defending his own and the angels' interests Lucifer pleaded at the same time the case of the recently created race of men whose station was so much more miserable than that of the angels. For all these reasons, Lucifer's action, erroneously called rebellion against God, was but a legitimate act of self-defense in the interest of the genus of the angels that their status might be redefined and true order and beauty be restored to the universe.

The advocate, knowing his client's pride and self-esteem, certainly would not have appealed to God's mercy; and for his own part he would have hesitated to take such a step because God was both prosecutor and judge in the case. The verdict, of course, was a foregone conclusion. Yet the defense had to be presented and its arguments thoroughly weighed to understand Lucifer's action.

Now we see Lucifer condemned as a rebel by the Lord and hurled into utter loneliness. The uproar has been silenced and the divine universe returned to order. The realm of peace and obedience seems to have been established for eternity. But it has not been. The true rebellion was yet to come. The manly and frank resistance, wrongly called rebellion, was to be followed by the real rebellion, the most formidable that can be imagined. This rebellion took place in Lucifer's heart. In the dogmatic version of the fall, Lucifer's nature does not change even after his damnation. But this was not so. When Lucifer found himself secluded and stigmatized for eternity, the unfathomable chasm that separated him from his legitimate aspiration suddenly became visible. His plight provoked the great and unspeakable reversion: the highest angelic creature transformed itself into the demonic being. In one decisive vision and action Lucifer embraced the Lord, His hosts and creation, denied their perfection and their right to exist and, with the power that was still his, vowed eternal war and hatred against what he had been and seen. The universe was shaken to its foundation and a new era had begun.

We see now a new interpretation of the nature of Evil. Lucifer's so-called rebellion has no relation to Evil. His action may be characterized as disobedience, as an unwise infraction of the established world order. We may even go so far as to consider it sinful, because we hold that a violation of the absolute divine will cannot but constitute sin. But even then, Lucifer's action was not Evil. A clear distinction must be made between Evil and sin. We are all sinners, we all repeatedly violate God's commands or, in fulfilling them, lack zeal and humility. For all that, we are not evildoers. If we were, the whole world would be the Devil's prey. Even that might be conceded, unlikely though it is, but the Devil's unconditioned reign over the world is likely to rest upon firmer support than the ocean of our petty (and even serious) offenses. If it did not, we would not have to surrender to Evil, nor would the Devil's pride be satisfied to get us at so cheap a price!

Evil was not born until after the damnation and the Fall. Until then Lucifer's nature remained uncorrupted. He had sinned, but he was not Evil. Again, we must examine the essential difference between sin and Evil. Their connection and alliance must not be denied. But to ignore the particular nature of Evil is to fail to compre-

hend its ghastliness. Evil is a permanent disposition of
the soul. It is a structural element of nature. Man is not
and does not act evilly at one time and good at another.
Evil is innate and influences thoughts, feelings, and
actions. It can be dislodged only by a miracle or by
supernatural intervention. Sin, however—if we abstract
it from the idea of original sin, which does not here enter
our argument—is a dispersed phenomenon emerging at
intervals, a temptation into which one may fall once but
not necessarily again. Even a habitual sinner is not an
evil man. What then is the nature of Evil? What is the
psychological and—if we may say so—the spiritual character of Evil?

Let us state first that Evil and sin do not differ as to
the quality of their intention and action. This sounds
contradictory and paradoxical and seems to undermine
any possible distinction between sin and Evil. The solution is this: no specific content distinguishes Evil from
sin, but there is a very specific attitude to the content
which alone constitutes Evil. It is the satanic pleasure
and delight in what is sinful, the unnatural enjoyment
and gratification of that which is contrary to God. Evil
has no *materia* of its own; there is no realm of evil
objects, actions, intentions. It is an attitude and disposition of mind and soul that not only works against all
that is good but also diabolically delights in the destruction of the Good. If a man murders his enemy physically,
or figuratively by destroying his reputation and social
position through calumny or false testimony, he quite
naturally derives a deep satisfaction from the planning
and the final result of his crime. But he does not enjoy
his intention and action because they constitute sin; on
the contrary, in all likelihood he would have preferred to
see his enemy removed by natural causes. In the same
way, when we indulge in sinful thoughts and fantasies,
we do not enjoy the sin committed. The saintly Louis IX,

King of France, who said that the only way to talk to a
Saracen was to run a sword through his stomach, certainly would not have enjoyed the sinful action of homi-
cide in itself. What gave him satisfaction was the idea of
discharging a duty pleasing to God. And the clerical and
secular lords who saw the heretics burning at the stake
did not enjoy the physical and spiritual agony of their
victims; they felt satisfaction that divine and earthly
justice were being fulfilled. Otherwise they would have
been seized by him from whose power they were trying
to snatch their victims.

Sin is, so to speak, one-dimensional. It is straightfor-
ward, no matter how involved and confused sinful
thoughts and feelings may be. Its satisfaction, emotional
and intellectual, lies in its technique and success. The
sinner does not get his gratification from the fact and
consciousness that he is committing sin. Such perverted
action and reaction fall to the evildoer, whose enjoyment
and satisfaction increase as the Evil he does grows in
monstrosity. The evildoer acts for the sake of the Evil,
and the Evil is nothing but the satisfaction and satanic
enjoyment he experiences in violation of divine and
human laws and values. The Evil is not identical with
these acts of blasphemy and violation, nor has it anything to do with the fact that Evil does not shrink from
the highest and the most sacred. It consists in the
diabolical satisfaction and enjoyment that fill the perpe-
trator of this violation and in the ensuing desire to
perpetuate the enjoyment.

At least one of the consequences following from this
argument must be mentioned. In view of the enormity
and perversity of Evil, the number of evildoers is likely
to be considerably smaller than might be believed. The
balance changes if we assume that a portion of the
sinners, particularly the nonrepenting, falls to the
Devil's share. This question must be left in suspense, for

there is no way to answer it empirically. But the implication is that it is by no means easy to be counted among the Devil's retainers. It would be surprising if it were otherwise. Lucifer appears as a majestic figure in the stand he took against the fatal test. Damnation did not impair his greatness nor his ensuing transformation into the Lord of Evil. It changed only from positive to negative. If this is true, then it is as rare a distinction to be among the saints of God or even among the blessed, as it is an infernal privilege to belong to the Devil's household.

Those who feel reluctant to follow this line of thinking must be reminded that the Devil even more than God suffered the fate of being dragged down to an all-too-human level. Few care, or dare, to ponder the idea of God and to arrive at a certain empathy with the spiritual image of God. Most of those who call themselves believers use their belief as a kind of coin to barter for the satisfaction of their needs. The difficulty of transcending the anthropomorphic God, who is inevitably a geocentric God, is almost unsurmountable. The Devil fares even worse. For there is every reason to minimize his stature, to make him appear petty and contemptible and to turn away from him altogether. And if it is possible to live in the presence of God because there is always the grace of His mercy, who can bear the vision of Satan in his abject majesty and still live? This perhaps explains the paradox that the Middle Ages, which cultivated, if not invented, the Devil as the formidable adversary of God, at the same time did everything to make him appear paltry, mean, and despicable. He was depicted as a similar human character would be, even in the smallest affairs of life, practicing his role as the great tempter by ridiculous means. In this way the Devil was dissolved into a host of subdevils and demons so that even the Church in her effort to fight Satan became more involved and occupied with his emissaries and agents, the witches and sorcerers, than with the Prince of Evil himself. In view of the virtual disappearance of the idea of the Devil in modern times, (now, however, being revived by the youth), it seems an honorable duty to reconstruct his true image. This image, however, must be completed by a feature as unexpected and astounding as it is momentous.

If Lucifer had turned into Satan by a rebellion against God, he would have been punished, and rightly so, by God. There would have been a clear balance. However, he was unjustly punished, because he did not rebel against God but only acted in protest against the status of the created being. Therefore the Lucifer who was damned was not Evil. He was punished for a crime he did not commit. Indeed, he may be said to have been punished for a quality and disposition he acquired after the punishment and as a direct result and effect of the punishment. He now fights God and His world with satanic lust and leadership, frenetically confusing, tormenting, and destroying.

Let us pause before the monstrosity of this spectacle. An uncertain suspicion suggests that the supernatural enormity and frenzy of the diabolical may hide a mystery as great as any we have found on our way: Can the diabolical mind, its dimensions and manifestations, be wholly understood unless it is assumed that a tiny spark of good continues to glow in Lucifer? Is the ghastly satisfaction in offending God comprehensible if every trace and evidence of good has disappeared? Is not some good, be it ever so deeply hidden, indispensable not only to keep the fire and passion of evildoing burning but also to render possible the enjoyment of it?

Still another argument: If the Evil were simply the negation of the Good (as the bad is), the presence of the Good would be entirely superfluous. On the other hand, the Evil, being the living, satanic opposition to the Good, renders the existence of the Good indispensable. Its presence is in no way actively effective. But even in its impotence, it suffices to incite Evil to ever new and increasing outbursts of hatred and disdain. It would be a grave psychological error to believe that the awareness of the Good in others could assume the same function and achieve the same result.

The negative argument, which shows that Lucifer could not have become Satan if the Good had left him entirely, is supplemented by a positive argument emphasizing the point that it was impossible for him to lose or destroy completely his former God-created nature. True, he denies and rejects his original nature, and his apostasy is radical, his will and intention are absolutely sincere. But we cannot conclude from his intentions that he succeeded. We might well ask whether the radical transformation from Good to Evil was in Lucifer's power. Everything speaks against it. He was the unconditioned master of his will, but not of his substance. He could poison the substance, but to destroy it was not within his power, and somehow and somewhere it remained what it was, though mute and incapable of acting.

Let us for the sake of argument admit the thesis that evil can exist without the powerless and speechless presence of the Good. What would be the inevitable result? Evil would no longer be Evil, but a negative, destructive power acting as straightforwardly and as naturally as the Good. The satanic Evil lacking constitutive momentum would cease to be Evil. No. It is the fight against every trace of good in himself, of which the Devil is constantly aware, that constitutes the deepest source of his ferocity and perverted contentment.

So we arrive at the last—but from the theological viewpoint, perhaps strongest—proof of our thesis. If God wanted to impose on Lucifer the most crucial agony,

what more could he do than to perserve in Lucifer this
vestige of former glory? Thus the Devil in torturing
others unwillingly tortures himself; but the fact that he
himself is condemned to suffer in the deepest recesses of
his being multiplies his stratagems to torment the world,
just as it stimulates the enjoyment of his own actions
and their diabolical fruits. It is because of this ontology
that he transcends the level of a purely negative and
destructive power and becomes a tragic figure rising to
the role of the great tempter and seducer.

Perhaps the reader who has followed the argument so
far will raise an objection here. Granted, he might say,
there remains something like a trace of good in Lucifer.
But would it not be more likely a mere recollection of the
Good, his former nature, than the Good itself? This
question is far from being artificial or merely sophistry,
and its answer would require the entire acumen of
scholastic philosophy. Fortunately the answer is not
relevant for our argument. The function attributed to
the remaining trace of the Good could be performed
exactly in the same way by the Good remembered as by
the Good existing.

Now to the final point of our exposition. The assumption of a spark of good remaining in Lucifer after his
transformation into the Devil and as the very condition
of his status as the spirit of Evil opens a view of
overwhelming possibility: that of the final reformation
of Satan, a return to his original glory. The conditions of
this transcendent event would be an act of conversion
and repentance on the part of the Devil followed by an
act of mercy and remission of God. The order of the
world above and below then would be restored for all
eternity.

This eschatological vision seems more in harmony
with the spirit of Christ than the official version of the
Church. True, this version is more dramatic and reveals

once again and for the last time Satan as the father of diabolical ruse and intrigue. Before the second advent of the Lord as the Messiah, the Devil appears as the Antichrist. In a last attempt to wrest the realm of the world from the Christ, he dons all the paraphernalia of an angel of light and sets out to overpower and seduce. His intrigue fails and he is hurled back to his infernal realm to remain there with the damned, for all eternity.

Surely this picture of the end of the world drama is infinitely more realistic than the traditional one. True, there is no indication in the state of the world and of men that the Devil has started on his way to repentance. But eschatology rests upon religion-based speculation and imagination in which the myth of a final conversion not only has its place but also can claim, despite a seeming paradox, an inner logic more in accordance with the spirit of Christianity.

It cannot have escaped the attention of the reader that in speaking of the Devil we must speak at the same time—all proportions guarded—of man. What is the Devil without man? A king without a realm. And what is man without the Devil? A brute without responsibility, without temptation, without the possibility of greatness.

Hans Holbein (1497/8-1543), From the CRAMNER CATECHISM

III

THE POISONED APPLE

Of the original manifestations of mankind's evolving consciousness, none is more portentous than myth. Hovering between the pregnant obscurity of the unconscious and the dazzling yet deadly light of consciousness, the myth preserves the intuition and wisdom that inspired religions and philosophies and will continue to do so as long as man does not resolutely turn his back to the realm of the spirit.

Of the many myths which have come down to us, the two most relevant for our problem are that of the origin of the world of gods and men and that of the origin of Evil. These myths, like all the others, form the bridge connecting the night of divining dreams with the creations of the dawning day. As they persist, they undergo the influence of reflective interpretation, which tends to disintegrate them and to obscure their primal shape. Such is the right and function of autonomous reason. But myth itself refracts reason's categories. Myth is neither right nor wrong, logical nor contradictory. It has its birth in another sphere where consistency, truth, and reality are measured by other standards. This sphere is intuition and experience; but, of course, it is the intuition and experience required by, and contained in, the myth itself. If we read with uninhibited empathy the Vedic "Song of Creation" (Veda X, 129) or any other great cosmogonic myth and permit ourselves to be carried away by the vision and the emotions it arouses, we reach a kind of self-sufficient experience.

The myth is inexhaustible. Seldom is its age, its birth-place, or its life span definable. But this does not mean that myth is ambiguous, equivocal, or deceptive. The incompatibility of contradictory meanings is character-istic of logic and reason, not of intuition and experience. The myth conceals many meanings, the interrelations of which may vary and appear difficult to understand. This is due to the fact that the myth stems from strata of the soul deeper than consciousness and therefore beyond the reach of our thought.

Myth is the source not only of wisdom but also of regeneration for civilizations. It may be asked why in our search for understanding we should knock at the door of the temple of myth in this age of science and sophistica-tion. The answer is that life has been molded and captured in numberless forms for many thousands of years. Yet we continue to seek solutions to modern problems on an *ad hoc* basis, having lost the power and capacity to ask the primordial and eternal questions with the innocence and directness that are the very conditions for the answers. For both questions and an-swers must transcend pure theory as well as the limita-tions of a particular place or historical epoch.

The myths upon which our interest centers are the fall of Lucifer and of man, and the origin of the world. The versions of these myths that have come down to us no longer are pure but have been vitiated by interpretations belonging to various historical periods. We have seen how stripping away some of these interpretations has brought us closer to the original source, if not to the original meaning, of the myth of Lucifer and his fall. The biblical story of the fall of man asks for a similar reevaluation.

A strange affinity exists between the fall of Lucifer and the fall of man. Both Lucifer and man disobey a formal command of God and both are doomed to pitiless punishment for all eternity. And in each case there is a highly debatable conception and evaluation of the offense and consequently of the character and gravity of the atonement. All these encumbrances are heavier, but easier to seize, in the biblical version of the fall of man.

In Paradise Adam and Eve lived in the state of perfect innocence surrounded by an animal life equally artless and uncorrupted. In this state the mere idea, let alone the act, of sin is unthinkable, even self-contradictory. The worst Adam and Eve could do was to indulge in foolish pranks. Even if they somehow abandoned the state of absolute perfection—of which there is no record —it was by definition done in all innocence and thus did not alter their condition. There was no place for real transgression, not to speak of sin and Evil. In this utterly defenseless state our progenitors were exposed to a situation of so mysterious a nature that it is doubtful whether it can be explained by God's expressed wish, by His silent consent, or by His total ignorance of the happening.

In this idyll there suddenly appears the serpent, which at all times and with good reason has been identified with Satan. How could he appear? If he lived there before, it was a strange kind of Paradise and certainly a defective one. If the serpent crept in from outside, the question again turns up whether it did so with God's permission and connivance, or against His will and without His knowledge. The serpent appropriately decided to tempt Eve. The desire for knowledge combined with curiosity proved irresistible. Had the serpent tempted Adam, it might not have succeeded. The indirect way led to victory. It certainly was not a glorious exploit on the part of the Devil. He did better later on in cases more deserving of his satanic ruse. But as a beginning it was perhaps sufficient. After all, what counted was not the way to victory but victory itself. And this was important enough, since it meant that his first plot against God had succeeded. He had forced his entry into the world of men, where his place henceforth would be recognized. This entry he forced not with the apple, but with the transcendent promise: "Ye shall be as God, knowing good and evil"—a temptation that would have proved irresistible to minds higher than Eve's. She, in her innocence, probably heard the words and some-how felt their inherent power, but her very innocence prevented her from even guessing their real significance. So she fell a victim to an all-too-comprehensible curios-ity. But to call this curiosity merely feminine indicates a gross ignorance of human nature in one of its sublime aspects, the insatiable thirst for knowledge.

It is difficult to understand how innocence could have prevailed against the Devil's foul scheme. Seldom has disobedience found more pardonable circumstances. There was, indeed, an almost irresistible compulsion to disobedience. And what was the punishment? One shud-ders in reading in Genesis 3:16—19 the anathema hurled forth against the culprits by a God of vengeance, a vengeance in glaring disproportion to the crime. It should be emphasized that fortunately the Old Testa-ment has not been influenced by the story of the Fall. It presents in its historical parts, in the Psalms and the prophets, a normal and intelligible relationship between God and man as well as between guilt and its atonement. On the other hand, the superhuman dimensions of the guilt were such that it could only be expiated and its dire consequences obliterated by an act of grace emanat-ing from an all merciful God. To the unique guilt, then, there corresponds the unique incarnation of God and His self-sacrifice in the person of the Savior. With this supernatural event, the world drama reached its summit. At the same time the abyss separating the God of Genesis 1 and the God of the New Testament was brought into the open and the differences were lost.

With all this, however, we still have not entered the inner sanctum. We have dealt only with the general setting of the Fall, not with its innermost meaning, the essence of the temptation: "Ye shall be as God, knowing good and evil." It would be easier to weigh the impact of the prodigious and ominous moment when these words were spoken if the central figures of the drama were not so glaringly out of proportion with the event. We find nothing of the greatness, freedom, and light we might expect them to possess as the only two beings God created in His own image (Gen. 1:27). On the contrary, we find a naked pair vegetating in unawakened innocence more like pets than independent and responsible beings. Then suddenly they become the object of a divine test and of a fiendish machination. The whole situation is neither diabolical nor dramatic nor tragic. It defies understanding. But this is not all. After driving the pair from Paradise, God "placed at the East of the garden of Eden the cherubim, and the flaming sword which turned every way, to impede the way to the Tree of Life." Again it looks as though the two unfortunate creatures who "shall eat the herbs of the field" might return to force their way back into Paradise. It is easier to accept the story if we forget Adam and Eve or consider them symbolically as representing the universal history of mankind in its misery and greatness, in its boundless levity and irresponsibility.

Paradoxical and abstruse as the biblical report must seem, there remains at the center this stupendous and demonic word of temptation: "Ye shall be as God knowing good and evil." Thus we arrive at the decisive question: Did the serpent redeem its promise? Did Adam and Eve know Good and Evil, and consequently do we, their offspring? There was certainly no one better qualified than Lucifer to know and to reveal the nature of Good and of Evil. The real tragedy begins here. And it is not too much to say that it has never been unfolded in its confounding complexity. The inevitable answer to the basic question seems to be that Adam and Eve did *not* come to know Good and Evil. Lucifer, the serpent, is the father of lies and could not but deceive them. But this assumption—the only logical one—is contradicted by God in Genesis 3:22: "The man is become one of us, to know good and evil." In this controversial issue the word of God must be decisive. Adam and Eve knew Good and Evil, so they had to leave Paradise, where such distinction was unknown, where it had no place. Lucifer for once had kept his word, since it was in his interest to do so.

The real issue now comes into the open. Straightforwardness is not the Devil's virtue. His ways are crooked and insidious, his promises equivocal and suspicious. He let Adam and Eve know Good and Evil, he opened their inner eye to the existence of Good and Evil. Why? So that in one shocking intuition they lost the blessed state of innocence and became aware of two irreconcilable realms; the one of Good, the other of Evil. With this fateful revelation, the Devil redeemed his promise but left man with a formidable knowledge that would breed nothing but utter confusion and fear. For of what avail is the knowledge of Good and Evil if there is no concomitant knowledge of their nature? To teach this, the Devil felt no inclination. Thus he kept his word to the letter and yet cruelly deceived his victims.

His dire success and the full meaning of his revelation quickly became evident. No sooner had Adam and Eve eaten of the forbidden fruit and become aware of Good and Evil than the loss of their naïve innocence couples with their new and terrible knowledge compelled them to look for Evil. Their eyes resting upon themselves, they saw their state of nakedness as Evil. Even if they had lived in Paradise covered with clothing, they would now have considered that state with the same feeling of Evil. This pitiable behavior was the result of their newly acquired knowledge. It compelled them to differentiate between Good and Evil without having the complementary knowledge of where to apply these categories.

This blindness and despair, this perplexity and helplessness, has remained the Devil's hunting ground. The Devil's first triumph was only a portent of success to come. The fall of man and his expulsion from Paradise begins the history of Western humanity, and in the course of this history, the Devil has proved no less efficient than at its dawn.

Henri Fuseli (ca. 1742-1825), An incubus draining a woman asleep, from *THE NIGHTMARE*

IV

THE DEVIL GOES
UNDERGROUND

The history of Adam and Eve is the history of man. Whether or not the event took place, the myth remains and, like every myth, it is not only eternal but also eternally present. We all are perpetually led into temptation and we do not stand the test. However, we need not cling too closely to the imagery of the biblical story. The eyes of Adam and Eve were opened to the truth that Good and Evil exist, that they are reality. They were shaken by this revelation and by their realization of the abyss. And, since no concomitant knowledge was imparted to them as to what is Good and what is Evil in their inner and outer world, the fundamental insight of the existence of Good and Evil, far from acting as a reliable guide, hurled them into confusion and despair— a satanic gift.

We, too, know that there is Good and Evil, but we also know their antiquity. We must accept the fact that we can have no unequivocal idea of Good and Evil, nor can we deny that in many decisions we find it difficult to distinguish one from the other. True, there is an unmistakable difference between our situation and that of Adam and Eve. We do not share their horror at the existence of Good and Evil. For we do not arrive at this knowledge suddenly, emerging from a state of pure innocence as they did. Moreover, in the course of time we have learned to compromise, to yield to circumstances, to become more "realistic." We have created an approximate idea of Good and Evil, of actions, intentions, and values that may be considered ethically positive or negative. Thus life staggers on, but the arresting question remains: What is the Good, what is the Evil?

There is no agreement among the philosophers. From the crudest forms of utilitarianism and sensualism to the loftiest ideals of self-denial and self-perfection, all possibilities have been exhausted in order to construct a universally valid ethical principle. On the other hand, ethical systems with a limited range of application have been invented to satisfy the needs of individuals or groups: the solipsistic ethics (Stirner), the ethics of the superman (Nietzsche), the ethics of the ruler (Machiavelli).

Among the philosophers who have formulated ethical systems professing universal validity, characteristically the wisest have been those who refrained from ascribing to the Good any concrete determination. For they were aware that any qualification could be but a limitation and therefore incompatible with the Good in its absolute form. Thus Kant defines or circumscribes the Good by conferring on it the form of a command, the *categorical imperative*: "Act in such a manner that the maxim of your conduct shall become universal law." And correspondingly the only determination of the good he thinks permissible is contained in his words: "There is nothing which without any restriction can be called good but a good will." Without considering the philosophical merits of this solution, we can say it contributes nothing to soothe the ardent desire of man to know the Good and thereby to recognize the Evil.

Plato is more flexible than Kant. All Platonic dialogues, whatever their immediate topic, center on the idea of the supreme Good, whether this Good appears as

God, Truth, Beauty, or Proportion. Approaching the problem of the Good with all the subtlety of dialectical art, Plato methodically closes in on the great mystery. But the veil hiding the inner sanctum is never lifted. There is no vision, no knowledge of the Good. This fascinating spectacle repeats itself again and again in the dialogues. The nature and existence of the Good closely resemble that of the myth without being identical with it. Certainly the Good exists, but where? Beyond any doubt, it acts and radiates, otherwise our nostalgic desire would not circle around it. And surely it must be definite, or our effort to pin it down to some concrete definition would be utterly senseless (whereas it is merely erroneous and inadequate).

The truth is that, in Plato, the Good, like the myth, exists in its own realm. It is inexhaustible in its significance, but beyond reach. Therefore the right attitude toward the Good is not knowledge and confrontation but infinite approximation. The irresistible attraction that emanates from the idea of the Good and challenges the desire to know it and the will to realize it not only proves but in a certain sense *is* its reality. This is the essence of the Platonic doctrine of the Good.

Thus the basic uncertainty remains: we do not know what the Good is. This ignorance cannot but work in favor of Evil. A twofold evil arises: Not only are we often incapable or unwilling to do what we have recognized as the Good and to abstain from Evil, but the Good itself as we consider it becomes an intricate and confusing problem. Our best instincts protest against this blindness. An indomitable desire urges us to strive for the knowledge of the essence of the Good so that we may recognize it in all its manifestations. This interior voice cannot be silenced by a questionable attempt to save the world by the evasive argument that it is sufficient for man to will the Good. It seems that egotism and self-deception withhold from us the clear recognition of Good and Evil.

Philosophy and science may find consolation in avoiding the fate of ethics. After all, the questions, What is Truth? and What is Reality? are strictly analogous to the question, What is the Good?—and they yield no more satisfying answers. Yet the history of philosophy and science indicates that, on the whole, ignorance has been a powerful stimulus and not, as in the history of ethics, a deterrent.

In ethics, ignorance of the Good produces a disturbing, even paralyzing, effect. Doubt then sets in and the Good is explained by or reduced to, custom, usefulness, right of the strongest, pity and so on. All these definitions of the Good are nothing but expedients. They single out partial aspects and specific components of man, but they do not embrace him in his essence as do autonomous Good and Evil. They are not only relative, dependent on history, on social conditions; they actually deny the genuine human person by dissolving his unity. Science might urge that ethics imitate the example of the scientific method in its search for a determinable truth and reality; and it might substantiate its negative attitude by pointing out that ethics possesses in man's conscience a specific and innate criterion of truth. But the voice of conscience, even when it speaks audibly and unmistakably, is hardly an infallible oracle, since it depends on education, and social and cultural conditioning, not to mention the limitations of the person himself. While not denying the existence of the voice of conscience, we doubt that this voice speaks the same language always and everywhere.

So we stagger on, lured ever more deeply into the tempting fallacy of substituting a form of group ethics— whether humanitarian, racial, national, or some vague convention—for an individualistic ethics. But no ethics deserves the name which does not place the human person in the very center of its considerations and demands and which does not tend toward the perfectibility of the person. Individualistic ethics may—and perhaps must—grow within a group pattern, but it must be peripheral to the group and never synonymous with it.

Group ethics easily can choke individualistic ethics. It is easier to recognize group authority in any of its various forms than to be an ethical authority in oneself. It is easier to do good to others than to discover what is good for oneself and to perform this good. It is easier to work for the improvement of the world than to work for the improvement of oneself, although the world would profit immensely if the inverse order were followed.

This catalogue easily can be amplified. The rapid spreading of anti-individualistic attitudes in the state and in society is in direct ratio to the growing unwillingness or incapacity of the individual to recognize the duty he owes to himself: to form himself before trying to form others. The history of man is witness to how difficult it has been to reverse this order. However, if we ever succeed we shall find ourselves in unexpected company. For the Devil himself is an individualist. True, he is an individualist in his own way, but that is his right. So, as we see, the Devil may appear when he is least expected. But whenever he comes, we may be sure that he will present a valid ticket of admission.

Pablo Picasso (1881-1973), *THE CHARNEL HOUSE*

V

THE DEVIL'S DISCIPLES

It may have struck the reader that in speaking of the opposite of Good we have referred to both bad and Evil. Bad can be defined as the neglect or violation of the Good. Evil is the deliberate outrage inflicted on the Good and is accompanied by a feeling of satisfaction. The counterpart of bad is Good, the counterpart of Evil is saintly; Good is to saintly as bad is to Evil.

Were it not for our arbitrary use of language, the distinctions would be clearer. We are accustomed to conceive of the Good in a narrow sense and to subsume the saintly under the common name of the Good, thereby obliterating the characteristic differences between them. On the other hand, we do not commonly subsume the bad under the Evil; and it is essentially an error to speak of Evil as a form of the bad.

To clarify those categories that designate fundamental moral values, the genuine pairs of opposites: "saintly/diabolical" and "good/bad" must be distinguished from the spurious opposites: "saintly/bad" and "good/diabolical." He who acts badly acts, of course, not only against the Good in the narrow sense of the term but also against the saintly. But the saintly is beyond his vision and his reach; it is the Good he deliberately attacks. In the same way, he who does Good does it in the face of the bad and is satisfied to deny and avoid the bad; the diabolical remains beyond his sight and his reach.

The Good and the bad are natural endowments of man. (This does not mean that they are by nature unconscious. On the contrary, they can and must become conscious so as to be lifted into the realm of the moral conscience.) On the other hand, the saintly and the diabolical are of a supernatural origin and essence. Both participate in an order which raises them above the moral sphere. Good and bad, however conspicuous their manifestations, remain within the proper order of morality. The saintly and the diabolical, however, reside on another plane, though they reach into and touch the moral sphere.

It is not mere pedantry to insist on clarifying the terms and elaborating on this pair of genuine opposites. They reveal unmistakably that in the great struggle between light and darkness on earth the most powerful adversaries and the only ones who are equal to each other are the Devil and the saint. To this the history of the saints and their own confessions amply testify. There we read of the numberless and various temptations, of the spiritual and even physical tortures, of the insidious acts of seduction—in short, of the entire register of diabolical art as experienced and depicted by the saints themselves or as reported by eyewitnesses and collected by faithful historians. The saints are well aware that any victory over the Devil is a triumph of militant humanity over Evil. And the Devil knows that every saint he ruins means a more substantial increase of his power and prestige than he would gain by catching ordinary souls.

In truth, the saint is the only game that can satisfy the ambition and lust for power of the Devil. For the Devil is a big-game hunter. Just as he tried to seduce Christ himself with a magnificent gesture in laying the world and its rule at His feet, so he steals into the souls and thoughts of the saints. Indeed, nothing is so deeply moving and at the same time shocking as the saints' descriptions of the ruses and arts the Devil employs to sneak into their most intimate thoughts, their devotional exercises and prayers; of the open threats he utters; and of the visual and audible fantasms with which he tempts them. These were titanic struggles, fought in the arena of the spirit. Had the appearance of the Devil been limited to this dimension, we would have been left a magnificent picture of man's fight with Evil—a duel in which the most powerful and refined weapons of mind and spirit were used, a drama so superhuman and yet so deeply human it could be fatally attractive.

The Devil, however, was not only interested in saints, popes, emperors and grandees and philosophers and scholars, where the stakes were high and the diabolical arts and temptations refined; he wished to lead everyone astray. There is an imposing list of luminaries who, for more or less substantiated reasons, are suspected of having made pacts with the Devil: Popes John XIII (965-972), Sylvester II (998-1003), Gregory VII (1073-1085), and Alexander VI (1492-1503); the Ghibelline emperor Frederic II; and Albertus Magnus, Agrippa, and Emperor Rudolf II, men who, during the Middle Ages, were occupied with the study of nature-phenomena in connection with ideas of magic. However, looking back at the history of the Devil in the Middle Ages, we see a steadily increasing vulgarization of the Devil. This process, particularly forceful and visible during the fourteenth century, culminated in the Papal Bull *Summis desiderantes affectibus*, which sanctioned the ill-famed and forever damnable *Malleus maleficarum*, or *The Witches' Hammer*, the bible of witchcraft and sorcery. Many were accused of witchcraft, and juridical casuistry and physical and psychological torture sent most of the accused to the block or the stake. This witchcraft and sorcery, and the insane accusations and horrors of the Inquisition, did not entirely cease until the second half of the eighteenth century. The number of witches and sorcerers accused of having made a pact with the Devil reached extraordinary proportions, as did the number of confessions, forced or voluntary.

No doubt, to create and to feed this greatest and most disastrous of all human aberrations, various motives had to be devised. Within the scope of our interest, only one, a psychological one, is relevant. We shall not discuss the superficial Christianization of the Germanic lands. Nor shall we deal with the repression of their pagan divinities, which survived as avenging specters and demons whose presence is distinctly felt in superstition. And we shall pass by the often-emphasized influence of the long, demoralizing periods of famine, pestilence, and warfare that turned people on to the Devil on the chance that he might have something better to offer, since, in any case, things could not get any worse. But let us just mention, to explain the longevity of this mental illness, the material benefit a good many people derived from the witch trials. The spies, the accusers, the investigators, and the judges all received high salaries; and the confiscated property of the condemned was turned over to the civil or ecclesiastical authorities. And, of course, denunciation was a convenient way to get rid of an enemy or a competitor.

But psychologically more important is another all-too-human factor. If we look at the persecution of the great heresies that started in southern France in the twelfth century and ended in the destruction of countless human lives and the obliteration of unique cultural values, we cannot close our eyes to the fact that it was the wealth and prosperity, the refinement of life and art, and the high moral standard recognized by the adversaries of heresy that brought about the accusations of heresy. Envy, greed, and uneasiness were leading incentives. They made people look suspiciously at popes and other high ecclesiastics, at princes and scholars. Such attitudes were instinctively defensive; they brought the envious compensation for inferior endowments or a modest station in life. Thus self-righteousness placed its own virtues in a stronger light.

Even more significant was a social trend of a general nature and importance. In the long era when the lower strata of society were the objects and tools of the leading classes, the cultural values, which were mainly of a religious character, came necessarily from above. Emotional attitudes, vices, and virtues, sank down and were eagerly imitated and absorbed within the limits set by the understanding of the lower classes. These limitations caused distortions in the values, resulting in a loss of distinction. And this is exactly what happened in the case of the Devil.

The pacts with the Devil made by the great at first were viewed fearfully. People crossed themselves and shrank from the enormity of the crime. But the example set by the great, the rewards promised, and the irresistible attraction of Evil could not fail to inspire the lower strata of society to seek access to the Devil. Devil worship began to spread. But inevitably with the change in the social level, the forms of approach, the cult, and the figure of the Devil himself had to change. The result was a sinister spectacle. Indeed the crudeness, the confusing superstition and obscene witchcraft testify to a degeneracy in which of necessity the Devil had to share. This witch-sabbath, though it could not wipe out individuals continuing the tradition of true deviltry, employed every device to obliterate them. In the Church itself, the situation was similar. There was a low level in the religion of the masses and in the moral standards of the lower clergy, especially in the administrators.

At the same time the religious genius unfolds in a variety of great and saintly personalities. This phenomenon, however, does not change anything in the picture painted above, namely, the popularization and vulgarization of the Devil and of deviltry. It would be a grave error to believe that the Devil himself had a hand in this evolution. Although it appears that the dissemination of satanic belief and practices would be heartily welcomed by the Prince of Darkness, what we discussed earlier in this chapter denies the probability. A power which looks at the saint as an appropriate victim of its intrigues and machinations would not be seriously interested in a devilish orgy of a proletarian character.

The Devil could not help feeling abused, misinterpreted, debased, even made ridiculous. But was there anything he could do to stem the insane fury? The logical, in fact the most plausible, conclusion is that the Devil withdrew entirely from the uncanny hubbub and left the mental epidemic to take its own course. This does not mean that he did not pick up victims who naturally fell to him along the way. But to imagine that the Devil organized the whole movement as a great crusade for Evil means totally to ignore his nature and stature. It means that one becomes a victim to a petty psychology, that of the witch-sabbath itself. This piteous humanity, despairing of the material and social conditions of life, tormented by repressed and frustrated desires, avidly grasping at anything which promised some alleviation of their misery, rejoiced in the feeling that they had succeeded in imitating those above them, perhaps even experienced a sense of pride that the Devil deigned to care for them. They were, of course, cruelly mistaken. The Devil paid no heed to them, and we can easily imagine him looking contemptuously down on this unholy uproar with a kind of satanic commiseration. Certainly he found no reason to quote the Latin proverb: *In magnis voluisse sat est,* "In great things it is sufficient to have willed." For there were but few independent and responsible persons to be found. And the Devil is indifferent to anyone anonymous, nor is he concerned with mass psychology.

Duccio di Buoninsegna (ca. 1278-1319), *TEMPTATION OF CHRIST ON THE MOUNTAIN*

VI

THE DEVIL'S LONELINESS

Lucifer before his fall was the first of created beings. If we follow St. Thomas Aquinas, angels are not only individuals but also species, a fact which ontologically distinguishes them from men. After the fall, Lucifer, no longer the first among the angels, became the genius of Evil. Formally speaking, we might be tempted to say he grew in stature, for by his own free will he made of himself what he had not been before. This, indeed, was his ambition. What he became he did not owe to God. Such was his *superbia*, his overbearing pride and ambition.

The angels are perfect in their way; they do not change. Lucifer, however, was revolutionary in that he wished to change. In that respect he appears more human because he took his fate into his own hands. Man changes as he lives; he mentally becomes more and more what he essentially is. As long as he does not evolve, he is, in a certain sense, not yet. With some people, life itself takes on the task of changing them. However, man should not be satisfied to be merely a plastic substance to be molded. He should take his formation in his own hands, or when life does it for him, he should at least by an act of free judgement and decision affirm or condemn what life has done and draw his own conclusions.

Lucifer is no paragon as far as the contents and

significance of his actions are concerned. But with
regard to clarity of will and firmness of decision, he
stands out as a great figure. He had been created a
consummate being, yet he wanted to form himself in his
own right. With us it is different. We start from nothing
and it is up to us to see that the raw material is shaped
and reshaped until it finds a satisfactory and final form.
Occasionally birth and conditions take the place of
personal effort and responsibility. But what is of interest
here is the difficulty connected with any serious occupation with ourselves and the dangers inherent in it.
These dangers are manifold, but two seem critical: mas-
sive egocentricity, on the one hand; disintegration, on the
other hand.

Creative occupation with ourselves forcibly places us
in the center of the matter. A process of contraction, of
narrowing down of the scope and limits of our being,
seems almost inevitable. Indeed, we need all of our
self-control so as not to lose sight of the fundamental
fact that we were created in a world, that we are not
without the world just as the world is not without us.
Any formation of the self neglecting a vigorous and
distinct relation to the world is not only defective but
dangerous. No need to emphasize that the world consists
not only of our physical environment. There is an objective world of nonphysical nature, too: the world of the
mind and spirit, the psychological world of other men. To
ignore this manifold world, or even to accept it merely as
an expediency that is useful for our self-formation, is to
expose ourselves to the danger of a shrinking process
that, under the illusion of fortifying the self and its
power, actually paralyzes initiative through unsound
introversion. What starts as a transcendent flight, ignoring or despising the way of the world, may end in
disillusion, despair, and self-torture. Here the Devil
finds an easy prey, not only because he has something to

offer—at least the illusion of transitory fulfillment and enjoyment—but because he and his victim share a preoccupation with their own importance.

The figure of Faust is not of the same order. Faust secludes himself from the world and men, but his insatiable thirst for knowledge raises him above ordinary circumstances and confers upon him superhuman magnitude. Contrary to the Devil's boundless egoism, the egoism of Faust refutes itself because he is willing to sacrifice his soul and eternal salvation for the attainment of his desire. On the other hand, it is doubtful that the boundlessness of his desire carries enough legal and spiritual weight to invalidate his pact with the Devil.

But this problem is of no concern to our argument. The various forms of disintegration likely to accompany an exclusive preoccupation with ourselves, clinically known as autism, are too well known to require description. Unproductive self-analysis, indulgence in fantasies which only in exceptional individuals reach artistic creativity, distortion of the picture formed of others—these may serve as examples. There is another form of disintegration which might be called empty altruism: the fanatic occupation with and devotion to others, their needs and desires. It is an altruism morally and spiritually without merit because it does not emanate from a well-formed, self-confident ego. Whether innate or acquired as the result of destructive experience, this empty altruism replaces and compensates for the ego's loss by living the lives of those to whom its feeling, thoughts, and actions are dedicated. This type of a disintegrated self, not easily recognizable but frequent in all so-called altruistic professions, is of no interest to the Devil, for there is no point of attack. It is genuine altruism that interests him—altruism sustained by a well-developed self—for that is a unique phenomenon which carries with it the potentiality of saintliness. Here, and in the sphere of the great egoist who like Faust wants to transcend himself in a super but not unselfish way, the Devil finds substance worthwhile to pervert and corrupt.

Having recognized some of the major types that are the favorite objects of the Devil's pursuit, we now must try to understand the techniques he applies to his potential victims. It may be illuminating to start with an anthropological observation of a general nature. Among all primitive and half-primitive peoples, the shaman lives apart from the community. Various reasons make this isolation not only desirable but imperative. The people themselves fear that the shaman's *mana*, or supernatural force, might be harmful to them. And the shaman himself has every reason to avoid the routine of ordinary life. Such intimacy could only diminish his prestige and profane his work by allowing an easy access to his art and its paraphernalia. More important, communal intimacy would disrupt his inner preparation, his intercourse with the power from which he derives his gift or through which he operates. So if he surrounds himself by an aura of mystery it is the natural result of conviction and experience that his exposure to familiarity is incompatible with his work. Thus his isolation is at the same time an expression of his mysterious powers, a protective measure and an inner necessity.

The shaman, the witch doctor, the medicine man are the ancestors of a long line of successors, magicians and alchemists, conjurers and faustian figures—in fact, of all those who from the beginning of history on any level of intelligence and education have relied on occult lore to obtain knowledge and power. They all live apart from the crowd, and their outward seclusion reflects their inner isolation, the one conditioning the other. They feel they must be alone to remain what they are and to achieve what they desire. In all that, they imitate—unconsciously, of course—their overlord, the Devil. Forthe Devil, as we said before, is enthroned in utter loneliness. We do not know how much he suffers from this isolation, or if he suffers at all. It is more likely that in his boundless self-pride he rejoices in the consciousness of loneliness and feels it to be in harmony with his magnificence.

These observations may help us better to understand the Devil's technique in seducing his victims. For this technique, whatever its trimmings may be—and they are elaborate enough—is essentially one of isolating the victim. The Devil draws—this is more than a metaphor—a magic circle around his victim, severing him from men and things that do not serve the purpose of seduction. Goethe, attracted in his younger years by studies of magic and occult philosophy, describes (*Faust*, Part I, Easter promenade) the way in which the Devil, in the shape of a black poodle, approaches Faust on his walk with Wagner. Turning to Wagner, Faust asks him:

> Watch how in wide concentric rings
> Near and nearer to us he springs:

and a few lines later:

> He draws an airy, magic coil, it seems to me,
> For future bondage round our feet.

Here we find symbolism and real magic combined. No clearer insight into the Devil's tactics can be imagined than in this description by a great poet. It only remains to be seen how they are applied and how they operate.

The man who gives himself over to the Devil must forgo both realization of himself and dedication to his fellow man. Any attempt at either is doomed because the

Devil will oppose it with new arts of seduction and distraction and, if these fail, with threats and violence. It must be said in all fairness that the Devil does what he can to fulfill his obligations. But there is the terrible restriction and condition that no positive attitude to men or things may be assumed. The result is the victim's exclusive occupation with himself which inevitably ends in an impoverishment and shrinking of the self. This is accomplished at the same time (but is concealed) through the immediate satisfaction of desires and the provocation of new ones.

The Devil knows that his worst enemy is boredom. This is why, from time to time, he withholds immediate fulfillment in order to increase tension and concupiscence. The victim ceases to take an active part in his life or indulges in merely sham activity. Caught in the snares of the diabolic plot, he is unconsciously isolated and hollowed. Indeed, unconditioned isolation and absolute sterility go hand in hand, and the immediate, or at least the assured, fulfillment of all desires paralyzes the will and deprives a man of a serious and useful occupation. The indirect relation to the self, which is the basis of a wholesome and productive life, is destroyed and the victim is dead before the Devil comes to present the pact and claim the prize.

We now strike a melancholy note. For almost everyone who sells his soul to the Devil asks merely for power, wealth, high position, or sensual pleasure—small coin, after all, for the service of the Lord of Evil. Few like Faust appeal to him to quench their thirst for supreme knowledge. The attainment of supreme knowledge is the only gift worth the price. But the granting of this desire is beyond the Devil's power, and those who seek it are diverted by fragments of scientific and occult knowledge, by hellish tricks and delusive spectacles, by an assortment of worldly and sensual indulgences* It can not be otherwise. For the only thing that the Devil can grant is the boundless power to do Evil. There is certainly a type of man, the true villain, who is the Devil's bodyguard. But he stands in alliance with his master and does not need to conclude a pact with him.

It is now evident what the Devil means by individualism: isolation that separates him not only from the other but from himself.

*The question often is raised whether Faust's pact with the Devil was juridically valid. Considered from this viewpoint, it was not legally binding, since the Devil made a pledge he knew he was unable to fulfill.

Eugène Delacroix (1798-1863), *THE PHANTOM OF MARGUERITE from FAUST*

VII

THE STEP TO EVIL

It is infinitely easier to fall into the Devil's trap than to escape from it. The will to withdraw and to discontinue the infernal relationship may be strong and sincere, yet the evil influence spreads so widely and deeply that more than ordinary courage is needed to extricate oneself from the Devil's snars. The Devil sees to it that his followers are constantly occupied, that they have no respite from faltering, doubt, and remorse. As the proverb has it: "Who tenders the little finger to the Devil, his hand he will take." Or still better: "You don't bid the Devil good morning before you meet him," meaning that you need not oblige the Devil beforehand; he will give you the opportunity soon enough.

All this is in strict contradiction to the ways of God. God does not permanently meddle with those who turn to Him. He remains aloof and is economical in His attention and rewards. The reason is that God respects the independence of man and his moral autonomy. He wants man to use his freedom to draw nearer to Him. What interference He poses assumes more the form of suffering, trial, vicissitude to test man's will to believe so that he may develop strength against temptation.

The Devil, however, has no pedagogical aims. He simply uses baits and promises mixed with sophistry to steadily weaken the will for the Good until, after a period of wavering and hesitation, the will for Evil takes its place. If the victim is not strong enough or wicked enough to take the final step that makes him the Devil's disciple, the Devil at least has the satisfaction of having caused the victim's personality to disintegrate.

To give an adequate impression of the Devil's nature and his foul deeds, it is almost impossible to avoid the erroneous impression that the Devil lurks always and everywhere. If this were true, life indeed would be a living hell. However, this most gruesome of all persecution manias is unfounded.

This applies equally to God. We cannot understand the omnipresence of God literally. Can we, must we believe that God accompanies all our actions and thinking as observer and judge? This idea is gratuitously distributed and mechanically repeated by many with deep conviction. However, it represents one of the most terrifying and perverted conceptions ever produced by the human mind. If we take it seriously can we comprehend it without shuddering in our innermost being? It may be comprehensible to the saint, who lives with and in God. But no other man can—or should—even try to live with the idea that every action, thought, and emotion is seen by God. Still less should he feel that God is his permanent companion or that he continually walks in the sight of God. Such imagination ends in paralyzing anxiety and fear, if not in utter confusion.

Some years ago the father-confessor of a nunnery in Ireland conceived the idea that God's omnipresence, since it is a fact, ought to be comprehensible and should be brought into the full light of consciousness. Realizing that we are mortals limited by our bodies and that the comprehension had to be adjusted to our limitations, he taught his nuns to imagine God as quasi-physically present in all they did and thought. The nuns obeyed— and within a short time were plagued by all kinds of psychopathological phenomena such as hallucinations, obsessions, anxiety, and fear. Finally, the religious authorities had to put an end to this phantom.

The story may seem all too simple, even absurd. Yet even today, through the use of health-defying drugs and magic and by consorting with demonic forces, modern youth is undergoing a similar experience. All of which proves that it is possible to be convinced of God's omnipresence but impossible to translate this conviction into concrete experience without running deadly risks. We may ask ourselves in all our decisions and actions if they are likely to please God, for this is but to appeal to our conscience. But the presence of God must remain an idealistic conviction—even a logical necessity—except perhaps in extraordinary circumstances which are the privilege of the few. As men we must enjoy the possibility of living life within wide bounds without feeling observed. To express it metaphorically, there must be a sphere of existence free from God and the Devil, although the dimensions of this sphere are not the same for everyone. This is postulated by the dignity of man, his freedom and self-responsibility. It is a privilege that, like all privileges, involves the danger, or at least the possibility, of giving oneself over to a colorless life of ease and comfort, satisfied to worship convention and to avoid the penal code. To the man of this caliber the words of Christ must be applied, and it is to be feared that such a man will be rejected by hell no less than by heaven. Indeed, it could be debated whether it is not preferable to fall into the hands of the Devil rather than into complete destruction. However, the real meaning and function of this idea consists in the freedom it offers to decide, either implicitly or explicitly, between Good and bad, saintly and Evil.

If the decision involves the first pair of opposites, one may feel satisfied with its finality without experiencing

the proximity of the principles of Good and bad themselves. But if the choice is between the saintly and the
Evil, the closeness to God or to the Devil will be felt. As
to the influence of the respective decisions on the life of
the person himself, no fundamental change necessarily
follows. There are good and bad men in all professions
and functions, and saintly and evil men in all strata and
conditions of life.

The decisions for the saintly and the Evil are distinguished by their confirmation in specific acts: for the
saintly, joining a monastic order and taking the vows of
poverty, obedience, and chastity; for the Evil, concluding
a pact with the Devil. Two distinct differences, however,
(in addition to the fundamental difference) separate the
one act from the other. The monastic vow is onesided:
the monk (or the nun) pledges himself to the fulfillment
of his vows, but God promises nothing. There is only the
well-founded trust that unfailing faith and the fulfillment of the vows will not be in vain. The pact with the
Devil, however, is a reciprocal contract in which rights
and duties of the contracting parties are clearly defined.

The second difference is that the monastic vow ties the
aspirant to a community or an order, whereas the pact
with the Devil separates the person from the community of men as a whole and isolates him completely. True,
there is the hermit who takes his vows implicitly or
explicitly, but he would deny the reason for his existence
if his love for mankind and the readiness to serve were
absent. There is no resemblance between his life as a
recluse and the isolation of the follower of the Devil.

It is not difficult to recognize the nature of the Devil.
And yet it is difficult for most of us to agree that the
Devil exists. At the end of Huysman's novel *Labas*, a
circle of friends discuss the fact that in our time belief in
the existence of the Devil has been deeply shaken. One
of the participants suggests that one of the Devil's

greatest stratagems is to deny his existence. Still, the suggestion is hardly enough to convince those who never have believed in the Devil's existence.

There is a third question which it is flatly impossible to answer even approximately. This concerns the scope of the Devil's activities, and particularly the degree of his success. In other words, what is the density of the population in hell? This is and will remain forever a mystery, so instead of indulging in useless speculation, let us summarize the moral and religious types of men and analyze the Devil's chances of seducing them.

The evildoer, as stated earlier, is the Devil's collaborator. But by an act of complete contrition and renunciation, he may redeem himself and become the stuff of which saints are made. As for the bad, they are the Devil's natural and most promising hunting ground. But the last step, the step to Evil, is psychologically the most difficult step to take because the bad man is instinctively warned against taking it. The realm of the bad is a realm in itself, as is that of the Good; and to cross over from the bad to the Evil is not simply to become worse but to change, to undergo a transformation in kind. One enters another realm, the Devil's proper domain. This, of course, is strictly parallel to the transition from the Good to the saintly, which is the Kingdom of God. Therefore, while we cannot deny the obvious affinity between bad and Evil, we must not minimize the inner difficulties consistent with the decisive step.

So we arrive at the sphere of the Good, and there we face an unexpected, almost paradoxical situation. The good man looks at the bad as his own polarity; it is the bad man whom he meets constantly. If he succumbs to temptation, he seems to move in the direction of the bad. Indeed, innumerable men who call themselves good sometimes indulge in bad feelings, bad thoughts, even bad deeds. Such slips are inevitable, since there is a gradual, almost imperceptible transition from Good to bad because they are situated on the same level and belong to the same rank, just as do the saintly and the Evil. Because the transition from Good to bad is gradual, and because the two spheres are on the same ontological level, the transmutation from Good to bad or from bad to Good rarely is the result of a firm decision. Almost always it assumes the form of a gradual and more or less conscious change caused by the influence of new contacts and surroundings.

For the same reason, the good man and the bad man are unlikely to hate each other. The good man rejects the bad one from the bottom of his heart; he condemns him, considers him an aberration of nature. And the bad man considers the good one contemptible, an obstacle, a thorn in his side. But genuine hatred is not characteristic of their relationship.

The relation between Good and Evil is different. There is no transition. The good man may become gradually bad, but he cannot become gradually Evil. If he turns to Evil, it can only be the result of a momentous, fully conscious, and deliberate decision. Indeed, if a good man with full responsibility takes the decision to betray the Good and work against it, he will not choose the bad but the Evil. He will not be satisfied to cross over to the bad; he will decide for the radically antithetical Evil, making the return to the Good practically impossible and enabling him to fight the Good by means infinitely more powerful than those available in the sphere of the bad.

The bad is nothing final because above it is enthroned the Evil. The good man is naturally attracted by the saintly. But once he takes the momentous decision to break with his past, he chooses the Evil, not the bad. The argument, however, does not carry the same weight when applied to the bad. The bad man, once he has resolved to sever the ties linking him with his sphere, is not likely to choose the saintly; he will be satisfied to change to the Good. The reason is this: the good man, even when he abandons his sphere, still retains enough of the energy to take the clearest and most decisive step; but the bad man is satisfied with the Good, which is on the same level, because it is easier to reach than is the saintly. The bad man lacks the impetus and, above all, the enthusiasm that easily, if not necessarily, goes with the Good. We see now why so many great figures in history make the radical and fatal decision for Evil.

There is no better illustration of this than the scene in the marionette plays of the seventeenth and eighteenth centuries when Faust decides to make the fatal step from Good to Evil:

FAUST:	(*to the six spirits*) I will examine your speed. How swift are you and what is your name?
CHIL:	My name is Chil, that means in your language arrow of the plague.
FAUST:	And your speed?
CHIL:	As swift as the arrows of the plague.
FAUST:	Your place is in the service of a physician. And you, the second here?
DILLA:	My name is Dilla, for the wings of the winds carry me.
FAUST:	And you, the third?
CRON:	My name is Cron, for I travel on the beams of light.
FAUST:	How swift are you, fourth one?
POMON:	As swift as the thoughts of men.
FAUST:	That means something. But the thoughts of men are not always swift; not when truth and virtue appeal to them; how lazy they then become! (*to the fifth*) Tell me, how swift are you?

LEVIATHAN:	As swift as the vengeance of the avenger.
FAUST:	Swift his vengeance? And I go on living; and I go on sinning?
LEVIATHAN:	That he permits you to go on living, to go on sinning, this alone is vengeance.
FAUST:	Ha, that a devil must teach me: And you, Mephistopheles?
MEPHISTOPHELES:	Insatiable mortal, even I am not swift enough for you.
FAUST:	Speak, how swift?
MEPHISTOPHELES:	Not more and not less than the transition from Good to Evil.
FAUST:	Ha! You are my devil! As swift as the transition from Good to Evil! Indeed, this is swift; swifter than that there is nothing!

Thus confirmed in our theory by the wisdom and experience of those who are proficient in the tradition of diabolic love, we may hold to the conviction that the Devil finds, if not most of his followers, at least his most distinguished adepts, among the Good.

The third possibility, namely, the Devil's successful attempt to alienate a saint from God and to add him to his followers, may be ruled out as extremely unlikely. No example is known.

Francisco Goya (1746-1828), *CONTRARY TO THE GENERAL INTEREST,*
from *THE DISASTERS OF WAR*

VIII

THE PACT

Having arrived at the supreme level of moral and spiritual existence, man may enter into a formal and binding relationship with the saintly or with Evil (for there is a negative aspect of the spiritual too). In the former case, this pledge takes the form of monastic vows; in the latter, it constitutes a pact with the Devil.

Apart from the fundamental difference in essence, there is a remarkable difference in the form of these covenants. As stated in the preceding chapter, the solemn commitment to dedicate one's life to the service of God is onesided because God does not assume any explicit obligation on His part. Nevertheless, it can be called a covenant because of God's presupposed *caritas*, His grace and compassion, which acknowledge the merits of His servant. Guaranteed success and reward necessarily would vitiate these merits. Nor does God seek anything for Himself; what He requires of man is simply what is in the best interest of man himself. The Devil, on the other hand, enters into a reciprocal contract of the ordinary kind where rights and duties are meticulously formulated. He insists on the formal and reciprocal contract because he wants something for himself, something that is detrimental to man.

But these covenants are not the only contractual relations between the spiritual powers and man. One

more must be added. It concerns God's relation to mankind and by its very nature throws into clear relief the
Devil's attitude. We have seen that in the mutual relationship between God and man, God, unlike the Devil,
refuses to deal with the individual on explicit and equal
terms. In spite of the explanation given above, such an
attitude on God's part might seem harsh and at variance
with his essence. But the fact is that instead of dealing
with individuals God prefers to make covenants with
superindividual entities. This He has done twice: in the
Covenant of the Old Testament and in the Covenant of
the New Testament. The first was concluded with the
people of Israel, and the second with mankind. The first
Covenant was renewed several times. In Genesis 9:15,
God said to Noah: "My covenant which is between Me
and thee and every living creature of all flesh...." And
in Genesis 17:7, He said to Abraham: "My covenant between Me and thee and thy seed after thee throughout
their generations for an everlasting covenant, to be a god
unto thee and to thy seed after thee. . . ." (although God
speaks directly to individuals—Noah, Abraham, and
others—He addresses them in their capacity as representatives of the Israelites.) In other biblical passages,
promises are made without mentioning the Covenant.
With the exception of Genesis 17:10, where circumcision is
expressly mentioned as part of the Covenant, the tacit
equivalent for God's momentous promise is apparently
man's acceptance of God as the only God and the necessary obedience to Him. Only after having defined the
Covenant (Exodus 19:5) did God impose the obligations
implied in it in a definite form and communicate these
obligations to Moses in the Ten Commandments (Exodus
20).

God's pledge to the people of Israel by His word
corresponds to the renewal and fulfillment of His pledge
by His deed, that is, His sacrificial death and His incarnation in the Covenant of the New Testament. Salvation

thus manifested and guaranteed by God demands in turn faith and transformation in man. Thus the Covenant is concluded between God and mankind through the mediation of the Savior.

The Devil does not recognize any reality other than the individual person; that is why he deals with him. All genuine communities, such as the family and those communities like religious orders which unite men by other than utilitarian ties, are a thorn in his side. On the other hand, the Devil is not opposed to associations and unions, such as the political state, which are founded on the power principle. From these he derives sufficient advantage because these forms of human togetherness are just as likely to favor the growth of the negative as of the positive in man. The Devil sees only individual men whom, in body and soul, he wishes to make his own. So, while the conditions of his pact remain the same, he will comply with the wishes and whims of his victims when it is in his power.

The pact with the Devil appears to be one of the most abstruse and preposterous aberrations of the human mind. Nevertheless, it is the strict and logical parallel to the formal vow of self-sacrifice and devotion to the service of God and, historically and psychologically, its imitation. In both cases we may ask why man, instead of feeling satisfied with dedicating himself with clear insight and firm resolution to the dispensation of Good or Evil, considers it desirable, if not indispensable, to invent formal ceremonies and institutions. Strange to say, such a procedure seems even less appropriate in the sphere of the saintly. It certainly is more difficult and more meritorious to lead a saintly life in the turmoil of the world and in the service of men than to live in the security of the monastery within a homogeneous community. If this is not commonly agreed upon, the reason can only be that, in principle, isolation as a form of existence is not in harmony with the Good and the saintly and that therefore the monastic community seems its adequate expression. It follows that it is not, nor should it be, the formal alliance as such that makes the pact with the Devil incomprehensible and abhorrent but, rather, its resulting isolation of the person from the human community. However, although the road from evildoing to the diabolic pact is no longer than the way from the Good or the saintly to the formal dedication to God, we face in the pact a paradoxical problem. To deny the existence of the pact, or to dispose of it as a pathological phenomenon, is as unreal as it is sterile. Indeed, we gain a deep insight into the dark recesses and processes of the human mind once we decide to approach this strange phenomenon with an unprejudiced attitude.

We know of only two original diabolic pacts, or what must at least be considered copies of the original covenants. The oldest book on Dr. Faust, published in 1587, contains the pact he made with the Devil. Though the story is but loosely connected with the historical figure of Dr. Faust, we may safely assume that the wording of the pact is in accordance with the customary pattern and in harmony with the rich popular and serious literature of the epoch concerned with the conjuring of evil spirits.

The two documents that have been preserved were written by Louis Gaufridy and Urbain Grandier (see pp. 88-89), both priests of the church. This, of course, is scant evidence to prove the existence of the pact, even if we add such well-documented cases as that of François Henri de Luxenbourg-Montmorency, whose pact with the Devil is said to have been burned after his death by his father-confessor, Rourdaloue. So let us approach the problem from another point of view.

It is unlikely that any written pact with the Devil would have been preserved, for the simple reason that it had to bear the signature of the victim written with his own blood and had to be handed over to the Devil. True, in the regular course of events, duplicate documents would be in order; but it hardly would have been in the victim's interest to keep a copy, because having the pact discovered meant certain death. Also the Devil did not want to run the risk of having his victim, in an excess of remorse, destroy the pact. So we may assume that the Devil took possession of the document and disappeared with it. In any case, a second copy in the possession of the victim was entirely superfluous. The Devil could be trusted to stick to the pact and to his obligations; only the victim might want to withdraw. So it was the Devil alone who needed a formal guarantee.

Under these circumstances, original pacts cannot be expected to have been preserved. As for the strange document in which Lucifer and his retinue specify their duties and determine the duration of their services, it may be seen as the elaborate product of hallucination. A mind starts from the current belief in the Devil and in a half-playful, half-serious mood, conceives the infernal document and finally, shuddering with cold fear, communicates it in writing and thus becomes a prisoner of the imagination's power. This explanation is perhaps easier to accept than the simple belief in the Devil's authorship of the pact.

Thus the pact is the outcome of a strange yet comprehensible psychological attitude. The man who wants to sell his soul is not in need of a pact. It is the Devil who must insist on the formal alliance, and if at times he feigns resistance and hesitancy, it is but a cunning maneuver to increase his victim's desire. All this anyone who deals with the Devil knows. Why then does the victim attribute such importance to the pact and show such eagerness to sign it? The underlying reason is that he feels the need not so much of engaging the Devil as of binding himself. The resolution to exchange eternal salvation for a few years of earthly satisfaction is so dismal and perverted, and yet the wish to terminate the infernal connection so compelling, that the more or less clear need to make the pact irreversible is understandable enough. This is the hidden psychological meaning of the pact. The Devil is obliging enough to act as though he, too, had to be legally bound.

There is, then, the almost inconceivable fact that man can deal on equal terms with superhuman power while he still remains bound to this earthly life. This awareness, more than any rewards to be expected from the pact, constituted for the Devil's greatest disciples an irresistible enticement and a prize for which no stakes could be too high. God, however, was far away. He did not appear and there was no immediate communication possible with Him on an equal and reciprocal basis. Certainly it was easier to have faith in the existence of God than in that of the Devil, but at the same time it was more difficult to feel His presence and to have palpable proof of it. The ardent desire to be in touch with God remained ambiguous and even unfulfilled; the relation was onesided, for God neither answered nor appeared. Not even the legitimate craving for an insight into the nature of the universe could be satisfied. The burden became too heavy. Therefore great minds turned in despair to God's antagonist. There they found themselves on solid ground. Everything assumed shape and was within reach. A formidable world opened, a spiritual world, too, but concrete and tangible, and one whose ruler and subjects invited a relationship based on equity and reciprocity. More than that, it was possible to attain mastery over these powers. For was there not a great and secret lore tracing their origin back to Eastern wisdom and perpetuated by men renowned for their insight into the magic forces of the universe?

We must try to conceive what the entry into the sphere of evil meant to those (they were of course the aristocracy) who withdrew from the Kingdom of God. No longer thrown back on themselves to explore the existence of God and how to become worthy of His presence, they now were free to follow a natural bent for living in a world that showed a strong affinity with the world of men. This transcendent freedom seemed comparable only to that felt by Lucifer when he dared to defy the will of God. Such freedom, fallacious as it later proved to be, did not remain merely theoretical and psychological. It translated itself immediately into real power. So, at least, it appeared to the man who, with all the devices of magic, conjured up the Devil and induced the Prince of Darkness to conclude a pact that made the Devil and the other infernal spirits his servants.

Interestingly enough, not only black magic but white magic—that is, the art of conjuring up friendly spirits, gods, good demons and angels—was practiced in the Near East during classical antiquity and during the Middle Ages. But no one in the Judaic or the Christian eras dared to conceive of evoking the existence of God by means of magic. This fact throws into clear relief the deep satisfaction which must have filled the mind of the Devil's conjurer who, paradoxically enough, seemed to possess power over his overlord.

The preceding analysis of the pact must now be considered against a general psychological background. It is well known that the ugly, the horrible, and the Evil in their extreme forms exert a power of attraction comparable, if not superior, to that emanating from the great manifestations of the Good, the beautiful, and the saintly. This attraction is not in itself unnatural or pathological. There is in everything that transcends the normal, apart from the interest such phenomena invariably create, a fascinating and irresistible power of attraction which may culminate in paralyzing a person, physically or mentally. If these reactions are not exactly normal, they are yet not abnormal in the pathological sense, since they represent the necessary response to extraordinary stimuli. The seductive power of the ugly, the horrible, and the Evil is normal so long as the possibility to reject this power is not jeopardized, and the reaction becomes pathological only when there is no alternative to these stimuli. For then it is not the innate power of the transcending force that seizes the mind but the surrender itself that fascinates and seduces with its foul bent for destruction, including self-destruction. This is the psychological source from which the pact originates and the soil upon which it feeds.

Texts of the Pact*

Text of Louis Gaufridy's pact with the Devil:

I, Louis Gaufridy, renounce all the spiritual and temporal goods which could be conferred on me by God, the Virgin Mary, all the saints of Paradise; particularly my patron saint, St. John the Baptist, St. Paul and St. Francis; and surrender myself, body and soul, to you Lucifer, here present, with all my possessions (with the exception of the validity of the Sacraments, in the interest of those who will receive them). Thus signed and attested.

(signed) Louis Gaufridy
April 30, 1611

Gaufridy was burned alive on April 30, 1611

Text of Urbain Grandier's pact with the Devil:

Lord and master, Lucifer, I recognize you as my God and sovereign. I solemnly promise to serve and obey you as long as

*Translated from Collin de Plancy, *Dictionaire Infernal.*

I live. I renounce any other God, and also I renounce Jesus Christ, all the saints, the Apostolic-Roman Church, its sacraments and all prayers. And, to commit as much evil as I shall be able to do, I renounce Holy Communion and Baptism; I renounce equally all merits offered by Jesus Christ and the saints; and should I fail to serve and worship you, and three times a day render homage to you, I give up my life which belongs to you. Given in this year and day: April 30, 1611

(signed) Urban Grandier

Grandier was burned alive August 18, 1634

Corresponding document by Lucifer ratifying the pact:

We, almighty Lucifer, with the assistance of Satan, Beelzebub, etc., today have accepted the pact that Urbain Grandier has concluded with us in recognition of which we promise him irresistibility with women, the choice of virgins, the honor of nuns, all conceivable distinctions, pleasures and riches. Every third day he will give himself up to fornication, he will indulge in drunkenness; once a year he will do homage to us and confirm it with his own blood; he will trample under his foot the sacraments of the Church and address to us his prayers. On the strength of this contract, he will enjoy during 20 years all terrestrial pleasures and after enter our realm to blaspheme God with us.

Given in hell in the council of the demons.
names and seals.

Hieronymous Bosch (ca. 1450-1516), *THE TEMPTATION OF SAINT ANTHONY*

THE DEVIL IN MYTH
AND LEGEND

Having examined the spiritual and temporal ties that bind together the Devil and man, we now will investigate his reality in myth and legend.

The Devil as a person is first fully portrayed in the book of Job, although the earliest myth of the origin of Evil and of apostate spiritual beings is found in the story of Genesis 6:1-2: "And it came to pass, when men began to multiply on the face of the earth, and daughters were born unto them, that the sons of God saw the daughters of men that they *were* fair; and they took them wives of all which they chose." The sons of God saw that the daughters of man were fair: angelic beings plunged into a separate and alien mode of existence. It is this rather than the story of Adam and Eve that is considered the origin of the Fall to sexuality, bestowing on it a horrible force. In Genesis 6:5, it is written: "And God saw that the wickedness of man *was* great in the earth, and *that* every imagination of the thoughts of his heart *was* only evil continually." So here we see how the universal sinfulness with which mankind seemed to be infected flowed like a dark turgid river from a single fount, namely, the unholy unions of angelic and human beings, and the commixture of mortal and immortal essences effected thereby.

"Satan" (Hebrew) means "the Accuser," and he accused

Job to God, bringing false accusations against Job, then urging God to tempt Job, to afflict him so deeply that Job will stop venerating God:

Now there was a day when the sons of God came to present themselves before the Lord, and Satan came also among them. And the Lord said unto Satan, Whence comest thou? Then Satan answered the Lord, and said, From going to and fro in the earth, and from walking up and down in it. And the Lord said unto Satan, Hast thou considered my servant Job, that there is none like him in the earth, a perfect and an upright man, one that feareth God and escheweth evil? Then Satan answered the Lord, and said, Doth Job fear God for nought? Hast thou not made an hedge about him, and about his house, and about all that he hath on every side? Thou hast blessed the work of his hands, and his substance is increased in the land. But put forth thine hand now, and touch all that he hath, and he will curse thee to thy face. [Job: 1: 6-11]

Interestingly, St. Irenaeus (*ca.* 125-*ca.* 202) in speaking of the Antichrist, declared: "Let no one imagine that [the Devil] performs wonders by divine power; it is the power of magic, since Satan runs up and down the world seeking whom he might devour." Had Jesus, for example, performed His miracles for the sake of demonstrating His messianic power, it would have indicated that He had capitulated to Satan, that He had surrendered His soul to Satan in return for the performance of the miracles. But the miracles were performed by Jesus because He fully participated in the misery of man, in physical and mental illness, in catastrophe, despair, and meaningless death. In a special way the miraculous powers of healing attributed to Jesus present themselves as the victory over the Devil, over the supraindividual structures of destruction, vanquishing the enslaving structures of Evil. Thus man may be redeemed (*redemere*), introducing the idea that Satan must be paid a ransom price for the liberation or redemption of him whom Satan has enslaved.

The personification of the Devil is found in many sources from the ancient world. For example, in Plato's theory of ideas we see that every form of existence, including lifeless things, has its archetype. This also appears in Plato's conception of the theory of correspondence between higher and lower planes, and of the astrological doctrine that everything in the cosmos has its star. The archetype is the special form of the noncorporeal, semidivine existence; it constitutes the deepest source of the soul's hidden activity and is intimately related to the occult and to the powers of prophecy and divination. Angels and demons draw their foreknowledge of human fate from these archetypes, as does the prophet. These mystical sources later expressed themselves in Christianity.

In a telling passage from the Dead Sea Scrolls of the Essenes one reads that Zoroaster, although never deified, created man to have dominion over the earth and made for him two spirits, that he might walk with them. These are the spirits of light and darkness, of truth and error. Thus every act (later taught by the Gnostics) played a major role in the universe as well as in man and could be attributed to either the Power of Light or the Power of Darkness.

Apollonius, the second-century philosopher of Tyana, relates the story of a young Corinthian who met, on a highway, a spirit which took the shape of a woman whose lover he became. But at the wedding banquet Apollonius denounced her, saying that she was a Lamia (actually possessing the head and breasts of a woman and the body of a serpent). Lamias had amorous appetities, but their chief appetite was for human flesh and they ensnared their intended victims with the bait of sex. They searched out young and beautiful bodies because their blood was fresh and pure. Lilith, the first wife of Adam, was accursed and she was driven from

Adam because she would not obey him; she was a dangerous lover and a murderer of children; later she became a
queen of the devils. This is the origin, in Christian mythology, of the woman of darkness who loves and kills.

In the New Testament, we learn from Saint Matthew
that a mortal sinner condemned to death by a high
priest escaped punishment in eternity. This, as we see in
the Avesta, constituted the "outer darkness" to which St.
Matthew alludes. It is a more merciful, Zoroastrian hell
than that of the compassionless St. Paul, who in I
Corinthians, Chapter 5, demanded that sinners be delivered to Satan.

The power of divination, the power of "knowing" the
future, can be interpreted as having beneficent or male-
ficent effects. Early Christian priests who possessed
such power were often successful in obtaining the highest religious offices. But some of these priests, who used
human sacrifices as a means of divination, were stigmatized as malignant magicians, and later writings by
monks portray these followers of demonic influences as
worshipers of the Devil. However, under the influence of
the Phoenicians and the Romans (who were in turn
indebted to Gnostic sources deriving from Palestine),
these priests became more enlightened and were able to
practice white magic as well as black.

Early priests often consulted a book at random (a
practice called "stichomancy") and sought to apply to
the situation the first sentence on which their eyes fell.
The works of Homer and Virgil often were used for this
purpose by the Romans. The Christians substituted the
Bible. The practice was forbidden by the church, but
priests standing in front of the alter often did it surrep-
titiously anyway.

The Devil, of course, appears and reappears in Christian tradition. He is so pervasive that even today in the
canonization of a saint and of his or her subsequent

veneration, a celestial prosecuting attorney must be present to provide reasons why the canonization should not take place. Hence arose the term *advocatus diaboli*, "the Devil's advocate," since this was the function of the Devil.

St. Athanasius (295-373), in his *Life of the Hermit*, wrote of Anthony's first strife with Satan. The Devil, he said, appeared in the form a dark Indian boy. Anthony, noting this, said: "Thou hast done well to appear in the form of an Indian, for thou art black in thy nature, and thou art as pitiably weak as a boy brought low by punishment." And in St. Augustine's *The City of God (ca.* 426), we find numerous examples of the various forms in which the diabolic nature showed itself in relations with men.

More than a century later, St. Gregory I (540-604) wrote of the nun who, forgetting to make the sign of the cross before eating some grapes in the convent garden, was immediately possessed by the Devil. In another story, a priest called to his servant: "Come, sir devil, and pull off my hose." Suddenly his garters became loose and his hose was pulled off by invisible hands. The priest was terrified and shrieked, "Away, miserable rascal (*Retro me, Satanus*), I was speaking to my servant, not to you." By which we learn, wrote St. Gregory, "that if the Devil be so officious in things concerning our body, how ready and indulgent is he to observe and note the cogitations of our soul."

About the year 1234, the accepted law of the Church in the *Canon Episcopi* stated that bishops must labor with all their strength to uproot thoroughly from their parishes the pernicious art of sorcery and malefice invented by the Devil. They were instructed to eject from their parishes any follower of this wickedness, for the apostle says, "A man that is heretic after the first and second admonition, avoid him. Those are held captive by the Devil, who leaving their creator, seek the aid of the

Devil. And so Holy Church must be cleansed of this pest."

Some women, it should be added, perverted by the Devil, seduced by illusions and fantasms of demons, believed and professed themselves, in the hours of the night, to ride upon certain beasts with Diana, the goddess of the pagans. Thus Satan himself, who transfigures himself into an angel of light when he has captured the mind of a miserable woman and has subjugated her to himself by infidelity and incredulity, immediately transforms himself into the species and similitudes of different personages and, deluding the mind, which he holds captive, and exhibiting things, joyful or mournful, and persons, known or unknown, leads it through devious ways. While the spirit alone endures this, the faithless minds of these creatures are corporeal, not spiritual. Who has not been led out of himself in dreams and nocturnal visions, and seen much when sleeping which he had never seen waking? Who is so foolish as to think that all these things which are only done in spirit happen in the body, when the prophet Ezekiel saw visions of the Lord in spirit and not in the body, and the Apostle John saw and heard the mysteries of the Apocalypse in the spirit and not in the body, saying, "I was in the spirit." Even Paul does not dare to say that he was rapt in the body. So whoever believes such things, or things similar to these, loses faith, and he who has not faith in God is not of God but of him in whom he believes, that is, of the Devil. For of the Lord it is written, "All things were made by Him." Whoever therefore believes that anything can be made or that any creature can be changed to better or worse or be transformed into another species or similitude, except by the Creator Himself, who made everything and through whom all things were made, is beyond doubt an infidel.*

*Cf. Charles Williams, *Witchcraft* (London: Faber and Faber, 1941).

We have seen that Urban Grandier and Louis Gaufridy made pacts with the Devil. They also claimed (perhaps falsely) to have been the first to say the Black Mass at the Sabbath and to sprinkle the gathering with the Divine Blood, while they cried: *Sanguis ejus super nos et filios nostros* (May his blood be upon us and our sons).

The Black Mass was celebrated by a banquet which was followed by promiscuous sexual intercourse. This often was extremely disagreeable. One participant said that it was as agonizing as giving birth; another said that the Devil's phallic membrane was scaly, and she suffered great pain. On the other hand, some spoke with pleasure of such caresses and insisted they preferred this manner of copulation. Others maintained that an artificial phallus was used, though that seems unnecessary, since the Devil, by one means or another, needs no foreign aid.

As part of the evidence against the Church and its periodic depravity, there is the history of a certain Madeleine Bavent. In 1625, at the age of eighteen, after being seduced by her confessor, she entered a convent at Louviers. There a Father David told her that God should be worshiped naked, as Eve had been in the Garden of Eden. As a sign of submission, all the nuns went naked to church and afterward danced naked for the pleasure of the priests in the convent garden. The priests then incited the nuns to make Lesbian love to one another, and to copulate, some playing the role of the male by using an artificial phallus. A Black Mass was then performed with every form of blasphemy, including, on one occasion, a nun bringing her newborn child to be crucified alive, then roasted and eaten. No aspect of lechery accessible to the vilest imagination of which man is capable was omitted.

The powers of Light and of Darkness are obviously a survival of the Albigenses' so-called heresy. In 1335

Catherine Delort and Anne Marie de Georgel were tried in Toulouse after confessing that for over twenty years they had attended Sabbaths and had copulated with the Devil. They maintained that although God ruled the heavens, the Devil ruled the earth; and that they were equal in power. Catherine declared that she had first been taken to a Sabbath by her lover, a shepherd. There she made obeisance to a great he-goat, then submitted to its and her pleasure. The goat, in fact, was one of the many manifestations of the Devil. The pagan Lombards, for example, "did after their manner sacrifice a goat's head to the Devil, running about with it in a circle, and, by singing a blasphemous song, dedicated it to his service."

The two ideas of God and the Devil, of Good and Evil, intermingle. Evil fell upon the world not because Adam's Fall actualized its potential presence, but because it was so ordained, because Evil has a reality of its own. Evil is by its very nature independent of man, yet is part of man, and is indeed an inherent element of the cosmos. It is woven into the texture of the world and into the existence of God, and eventually of man himself. Evil may be said to be a sort of residue or refuse of the hidden life's organic process. Evil becomes evil when something which is good in its right place tries to usurp a place for which it is not fitted.

Thus man's sinfulness actualizes the potentially evil and causes it to tear itself away from the divine. The Devil always destroys a union, and a destructive separation of this kind was immanent in the original sin through which the fruit was separated from the tree. The Tree of Life was separated from the Tree of Knowledge, man forgetting that both of these trees have one and the same root. Therefore, if man falls into this segmentation, this alienation and isolation; if he seeks to maintain his own self (the contemporary problem of concern of our youth of today) instead of remaining in the original context of all created things (in which he, too, has his legitimate place), this act of apostasy bears fruit in the demiurgical presumption of magic, demonology, and deviltry in which man seeks to take God's place (as the Devil did). Evil then creates a world of false contexts after having destroyed or deserted the Good.

The separation of the qualities of strict justice and moral judgment in and by God from the harmonious whole, from their true interrelationship, from their sacredness and the Good—such separation becomes the cause of Evil. There is the quality of wrath on the one hand of God, and the quality of mercy and love on the other hand of God. And one cannot manifest itself without the other. Thus the great fire of wrath which burns in God is often tempered by His mercy. But when it ceases to be tempered, when in its hypertrophic tearing itself away from the quality of mercy, then it is transformed into that which is radically evil; it becomes the Devil incarnate and belongs to the dark world of Satan.

We then come to the inevitable conclusion that Evil exists in order to increase man's choices and his opportunities. This leads us to the question of freedom. Man has freedom and will in order that he may have the possibility of overcoming the dark satanic forces and prove his moral strength to transmute Evil into a spiritual and moral triumph.

Nevertheless, it must never be forgotten that although satanic power may be banned, or even temporarily overcome, it never can be completely eradicated; it always will return in one form or another. In somewhat less mythological language we can say that it is certainly true that the satanic forces in the universe, as in man, can be positively conquered in a special place and in a special time, but they never can be totally banished from reality, since reality consists of both Evil and Good in a complimentary coexistence. This means that all utopian movements possess an inherent and genuine warning against utopianism. The Devil may be subdued for a time, but the Devil is not dead. To realize this truth is man's burden and his greatness, as we shall see.

Lorenzo Maitani (ca. 1275-1330), *THE INFERNO*

X

THE DEVIL'S IMAGE

The question whether our conception of the Devil as the great opponent of God is the only one possible need not concern us here. As long as the Devil is believed to argue with God and to arrogate to himself unlimited sway over the world and men, his appearance, nature, and success depend upon our idea of God and the character of God's leadership.

The God of the Old Testament, in the period before the Hebrew prophets, was an Almighty Patriarch, well conscious of His power. In general He was intent on the welfare of His tribe, later His people; but now and then, as anyone in His place would do, He used his power arbitrarily. Yielding to His caprices, He became at times unjust and acted against His own principles. He was a jealous God bent on the maintenance of His prerogatives and prestige. He meant well, but He was easily irascible and indulged in His unpredictable moods. He had His favorites and His pronounced inclinations and aversions, of which Cain and Abel are the first outstanding examples. All in all, He was not an unkind God. On the contrary, He was amiable, especially in view of His age, His power, and His unmistakable good intentions.

He claimed to be the only God and insisted on being recognized as such, even in the face of heated competition. For the texts do not always make it clear whether

He flatly denied the existence of other gods or was satisfied with stating their impotence and uselessness. In reality this question was not of much interest to Him, since His only ambition and pretension was to be the God of Israel. Only the prophets transcended this limitation.

The most important fact, however, is that this God cannot be designated as absolutely good or identified with the idea of Goodness. Indeed, He himself does not lay claim to this designation. His essential, unique, and grandiose pretension is not of a moral nature; it is ontological: I am who I am. In this majestic form, unequaled in weight, simplicity, and clarity, He announces and defines himself. Nothing else, real or imaginable, reaches into the sphere where essence and existence are one and where being coincides with doing. He *is*. Here is absolute authority inherent in absolute being. Let there be no doubt. At that moment of the history of the Jews it was infinitely more important to reveal to those poor nomads, who had lost their home and were searching for another, the bare fact that there is a God, one God, their God, than to come forward with a god of utter perfection and goodness—qualities that were beyond the comprehension of a people who had just escaped from slavery. A God with such attributes only would have been exposed to misinterpretation and misuse. Indeed, when we remember what Moses expected his people to understand and to achieve, their lapse into idolatry, disobedience, and offenses of all kinds seems inevitable and indicates that not even this stern and uncompromising figure of God commanded sufficient authority. What would have happened if an indulgent and all-merciful God had been revealed? Nothing but confusion and contradiction. This is why God, whenever He stresses His mercy, never forgets to add the stern warning addressed to the transgressors of the law in

Exodus 34.6: " . . . merciful and abundant in goodness and truth; keeping mercy unto the thousandth generation, forgiving iniquity and transgression and sin; and that will by no means clear the guilty; visiting the iniquity of the fathers upon the children and upon the children's children, unto the third and unto the fourth generations."

All this is not surprising; it is natural enough. We have only to remember the Decalogue in order to stand in silent admiration of what could be revealed to and imposed upon a people least prepared to receive the divine message and to carry the burden of its fulfillment.* God had to be vindictive, and His reactions sometimes had to be unpredictable to hold the people in awe; but even this method did not always succeed. The idea of the one God distributing Good and Evil could be understood and assimilated only at the price of long and severe exertions, tribulations, and humiliations. The God of the prophets was the reward.

The one God, once He had decided to reveal himself under the extraordinary circumstances He chose, could not appear other than as He did. As stated above, it was important to insist on the fact that He *is* rather than to show *what* He is. The unfolding of His essence could wait; the unambiguous positing of His existence could not. The one God did not immediately appear as *the* Good; still less as the perfect or as love; nor even as unconditional and intelligible justice.

Remembering that the Devil is the opponent and adversary of God as the absolute Good, it is easy to understand that the God of the Old Testament is sufficiently distant from the absolute Good to dispense with the idea of an independent negative power. What there

*There is no comparison of this revelation in the law codes of Hammurabi nor in the strictures of other Near Eastern kings.

was or seemed to be of Evil in the world could be explained by the ill-will and misdeeds of men or interpreted as revenge and punishment or as a visitation sent by God. Satan, in the book of Job, lacks any characteristic of the satanic. At the beginning of the book he presents himself before the Lord "among the sons of God." He is one of God's agents—not even an accuser but a tempter, with God's explicit permission. In the performance of his duties he carries out his plans approved by God, and the satisfaction he feels with the task well done has no relation whatever to the satanic enjoyment of the Evil inflicted and the pain suffered by the victims. In Judaism, the Devil never transcended this clearly circumscribed role of a faithful servant of the Almighty. However, it is important to remember that the belief in a world of demons, good and bad, as it developed particularly in the Mesopotamian civilizations and in later Zoroastrianism, penetrated into the popular religion of Judaism and, later, tinged Christianity. The Jews of the Diaspora and the spreading Christianity carried the belief in demons and the corresponding magic arts to Europe. Hence the names of many demons in medieval magic literature betray their Hebrew origin, while a few learned rabbis were reported to be masters of the black art.

There is no trace of the true Devil as an autonomous power and the antithesis of God either in the Old Testament or in later Judaism. In the construction of the real Devil, the influence of the Zoroastrian principle of Evil, Angru Mainyu, is more than probable. But it is infinitely more important to recognize the inner necessity in the New Testament that demanded the perfect formation of the diabolic power. The evolution of Greek philosophy placed the authors of the Gospels in a different intellectual atmosphere. God was conceived as the absolute Good in harmony with Plato's Supreme Idea. But, contrary to philosophy, where the Supreme Good remained aloof and beyond experience, accessible only to the rare vision of a Plotinus, religion was entitled to demand a concretization of the idea of the Good that made it visible to the eyes of the many and a guarantee to those who desired to actualize it in their own souls. Thus the absolute Good took shape in the person of Christ.

This, however, represents only one aspect of the new situation. The other is of greater significance for our argument. With the glaring manifestation of the absolute Good, it no longer was possible to varnish the Evil with halfhearted explanations and tergiversations. It had to be faced for what it was: the strict opposite of the Good, an absolute in its own right. Thus the Evil became a true absolute, not only the lukewarm negation of the Good, but its irreconcilable enemy, personified in a great, war-like figure confronting God himself: the Devil was born.

It is a problem of metaphysics whether there can be two absolutes—in other words, whether the concept of an absolute does not by definition preclude a dualism. But what represents a problem in philosophy may be true in religion. What must be emphasized is the fact that the dualism of God and Devil is strictly against the spirit of the Old Testament.

The dialectic postulate that one extreme presupposes the other had been satisfied, and the Devil took possession of his throne in great pomp and with all the paraphernalia of his power. The difficulties and dangers resulting from this enthronement are clearly visible in the writings of the early Fathers of the Church. The question of how God could admit Evil without avoiding Gnostic dualism and its doctrine of the good God and the evil creator and ruler of the world; the question of how the Devil's legitimate claim to the souls of men derived from original sin as being compatible with the sacrificial death of Christ and its redeeming power; the question whether the final conversion of the Devil as advocated by some of the Early Church Fathers, if it happened at all, would annul dualism; the major problem how the Manichaean doctrine, according to which all existence is divided into the two fundamentally different and antagonistic spheres of Good and Evil, could be refuted. In all such questions, theological wisdom and subtlety had to stand the test. Theology had to preserve Evil and the Devil, and at the same time prove God's omnipotence and goodness. Theology had to explain the meaning and purpose of Evil and at the same time ensure man's free will and his chance of salvation. While theology was absorbed in these problems, the terrestrial and the supernatural world were filled with the hosts of the Devil seeking the downfall of man.

Greek thought had impregnated and shaped the new religion, and in the process it had placed before it almost insoluble problems. At the same time, the belief in angels and demons penetrated into the new creed from the syncretistic religions of the Near East, including popular Judaism. Among them the figure of the Devil had risen to unique prominence because the absolute Good required the incarnation of absolute Evil. However, this incarnation attained full efflorescence and vigor only when the emperor Constantine I made Christianity the religion of his empire. Then the pagan creeds—particularly those of Europe, and among them the pantheism of the Slavs, the early Germans, and the Celts, with their rich worlds of gods and spirits—were transformed from one day to the next into a pandemonium as a result of their conversion which was enforced by the sword. Characteristically enough, these deities and spirits were debased to demons, and the Devil's retinue lived on for centuries, their reality recognized by the religious authorities. "Pagan" became synonymous with "devilish," and through this identification the power of the Devil increased in the following centuries. His presence was seen and felt everywhere, in the numerous heretical sects no less than in the trifling mishaps of daily life. And this fear did not respect rank or reputation.

It is noteworthy that in the epochs preceding the fourteenth century—a period of rare efflorescence in personal devoutness and theological scholarship as well as in achievements in the arts—the fear of the Devil and his hosts in the crudest forms of superstition penetrated not only the masses but the intelligentsia, both clerical and secular. What emerges in the persecution of the heretical sects in France or the order of the Templars and in the trials for witchcraft and connivance with the Devil surpasses anything that credulity and imagination or religious fervor and sadism have produced anywhere or at any time. But disregarding the human, mean, and vicious motives that are inseparable from the history of the Inquisition; the fanaticism and thirst for power and wealth; the lust for personal revenge; and the stupidity and superstition—there is also a sadly logical incentive in some persons to indulge in the orgy of torture and slaughter that delivered up untold thousands of men, woman, and children to the block and the stake, an incentive that originated from a deep, if misled concern for the preservation of the pure faith and the protection of the true believers.

It is perhaps not an exaggeration to say that in this period the fear of the Devil preoccupied minds more effectively than the love of God. For when fear has reached a certain depth it exerts a paralyzing influence that surrenders man helplessly to the object of his fears. And since fear is more contagious than any other emotion, the fear of the diabolic forces increased to proportions that made it the most formidable mass epidemic in history. This phenomenon was met with countermeasures taken by the Church with the assistance, more or less, of the secular authorities.

The situation must be understood in its fullness to appreciate its immediate consequences. On all sides the Kingdom of Evil bordered the realm of the Good. With every increasing cunning and ruse, the legions of the Devil worked their way into the world of God. There was no neutral ground between them. The broad zone of agnosticism, indifference, doubt and critical examination, simple ethics and reason that later became so strong and important did not exist; nor could apathy be tolerated. "He who is not for me is against me" was the watchword of the day. He who did not firmly stand with the Church was inevitably the Devil's accomplice. There being nothing between the two, a clear decision had to be made; indifference to the Church was considered adherence to Satan. Since the clash between the two was not being cushioned by any shock-absorber, the Church in its defensive position had to have recourse to extreme measures, and so it did.

The theoretical crystallization and expression of this demonomania is the ill-favored *Witches' Hammer,* the formidable product of morbid hallucination, delusion, and madness that owed its origin to German vigor, violence, and organizational talent. Published in 1487, *The Witches' Hammer* is based on the 1484 Papal Bull *Summis desiderantes affectibus,* in which Pope Innocent VIII, on the instigation of the two German inquisitors, Jacob Sprenger and Heinrich Justitoris, solemnly recognized the danger of witchcraft and sorcery in union with the Devil and made legal the suppression and eradication of the Evil by all appropriate means. This mental epidemic did not begin to subside until the seventeenth century. Even so, witchcraft and sorcery did not disappear from the criminal codes of the European states until the second half of the eighteenth century.

An enormous display of energy and courage, acumen and self-sacrificing were required to inaugerate and maintain the fight. It had to be proved not only that the superstitious belief was incompatible with Christianity but also that it contradicted reason and experience; and for this purpose, natural explanations and interpretations of the pertinent phenomena had to be found. Men like Johann Weier in the sixteenth century; Gabriel Naudé, Balthasar Bekker, Christian Thomasius, and many others in the seventeenth century—men who were Protestants, or were tinged by the new science of nature —were connected with the spiritual and intellectual revolution. And a revolution it was, no less than the Enlightenment of the eighteenth century. Indeed, this period might be called the true Enlightenment because it signified in a deeper sense than that of the eighteenth-century a purification of soul and mind. We preceive the eighteenth century Enlightenment because it evolved with logical necessity and its influence spread from the realm of ideas to political and social issues. But the fire had been kindled earlier and its light made the Enlightenment possible.

Such is the general background against which the appearance and disappearance of the Devil must be understood. Against this background, the figure of the Devil as it developed in the countries north of the Alps, in Germany, northern France, England, and some smaller countries, stands out in clear relief.

The Near and Middle East is the classic source, for the Western world, of the hilt of religions. Within the multiplicity of coexisting and succeeding religious movements that originated in these areas, none attracted particular attention on its own merits. Thus the newborn Christian creed was but one of the many mystery religions that spread within the Roman empire and found its way to Rome. We know that the cult of the Persian god Mithra

came within a hair's breadth of being made the religion
of the Roman empire and thereby of the Western world.
The coexistence within the empire of numerous creeds
was a fact, and a change from one to the other was
common. Thus, when Constantine declared the religion
of the Christ to be the religion of the state, what was
shocking was not so much that this particular creed, but
that *any one* religion, had been made official. The fact
that Christianity was at the time hardly among the
socially prominent religions only added to the conster-
nation.

The situation in northern Europe, however, was entirely different. There Rome never had secured a foot-
hold, as it had in northern Germany, the Slavonic regions
of Prussia, northern England, and Ireland. There, in
southern England and in the regions of what are now
Holland, Belgium, and the north of France, as a result of
the weakening of the central power and the continuous
battling on the eastern frontiers of the empire, the
Roman garrisons had to be withdrawn. There the indige-
nous ancestral religions continued to live on: the gods of
the Slavs, the Germans, and the Celts.

The new religion had come to these regions through
the zeal of missionaries in the most efficient mission:
compulsory conversion as the result of military subjection. Strangely enough, it was, at least on the European
mainland, the Germanic tribes who assumed the task of
ecumenizing the new creed. Having penetrated into
Roman territory, they established themselves and, with
a varnish of Roman civilization, embraced the Christian
dogma. Later, breaking away from the empire, they
returned to their former habitats and even moved into
adjacent regions that in the meantime had been popu-
lated by newcomers in the course of the great migra-
tions. Wherever the Germanic tribes went, forceful conversion, accompanied by bloody massacres of those who

resisted, marked the way of the victors, the best-known example being the subjection and conversion of the Saxons by Charlemagne.

The psychological circumstances in which the Nordic people suddenly found themselves differed radically from those in the Mediterranean regions. Deeply rooted in their own never-contested faith, unacquainted with religious subtleties, the people had to face a strange and to them abhorrent creed upheld by the force of arms, a creed in which the new deities—God, Christ, and the Virgin—bore no relation to those they had worshiped before. In contrast to the religious experience of the Orientals, the Greeks, and the Romans of that period, the Germanic tribes lacked a center of assimilation. The new religion came as a catastrophe of nature. It threatened to destroy what had been held sacred and eternal. Superficially, within the realm of consciousness, the conversion was a rapid and unlimited triumph. Not so in the twilight of consciousness, nor in the dark depths of the subconscious. There the old gods continued to live. True, they lived degraded and stigmatized by the new creed. They were held to be evil spirits and demons; but this official mark of disgrace was not strong enough to dispossess them. Characteristically, we find the old deities in tales and legends as benevolent figures. But most important is the fact that neither the victors nor their priesthood dared to doubt the existence of the newly created or discovered evil spirits and demons. In the newly created netherworld, the Devil was readily admitted. He found there an impregnable fortress and many ready helpers. Indeed, the priesthood often thought it prudent to protect themselves by mass and prayer before they dared to smash idols or destroy temples.

All this followed because the new religion was grafted and forced upon vigorous, but culturally and intellectually immature, people. It was only natural, therefore, that the new pseudo-Christians in a more or less conscious turn withdrew to the cherished sanctuary of their innermost recesses. Professing openly the new creed but in reality fearing and rejecting it, they remained more or less consciously devoted to the old legacy under whatever form it presented itself—as always happens in a true union.

We can see now that the vehement and irresistible belief in the Devil and his hosts, the delirium of witchcraft and black magic, must be understood as the direct and inevitable outcome of an imposed foreign creed. It is the psychologically justified and necessary revenge of the lacerated soul of a people forced into a paradoxical situation, a revenge all the more tragic because ultimately, in the witchtrials, they themselves had to pay the price.

Pablo Picasso (1881-1973), *THE DREAMS AND LIES OF FRANCO I*

XI

THE FEAR OF THE DEVIL

The peoples upon whom the new God had been imposed at the point of the sword had every reason to fear and to hate Him, none to love Him. He had caused the destruction of all they had worshiped and the death of those who had resented Him. To love Him they had much to forget. But the hidden memory of closely united peoples is very powerful and works more efficiently the greater the effort made to obliterate it. It does not even depend upon facts. They may vanish; but the psychological dynamics, the subconscious attitudes connected with the facts—these constitute the true reality, which survives anonymously.

Such psychological dynamics exert an influence counter to the general overt belief, so these violent undercurrents obstructed and delayed the assimilation of the new creed. After more than a thousand years (taking the reign of Charlemagne as the point of departure), the situation has become normal; but it still remains uncertain whether the old gods transmuted by Christianity have been successfully absorbed and finally silenced.

During the greater part of this critical millennium, God was certainly more feared than loved. This fear was primitive fear, the natural apprehension of an overwhelming invisible power; it had little to do with the true fear of God, which is veneration and awe—the only kind of fear that can coexist with the love of God. There is no doubt that the love of God can reach proportions that can eradicate any kind of fear. On the other hand, God may be worshiped in awe and veneration without any feeling of love. The union of true religious fear and love of the Godhead as it is found in Christianity and fully developed Judaism represents a high and rich form of spirituality. The ancient Greeks, Romans, and the peoples of the Near and Middle East generally feared their gods, but they did not love them. They confronted the beneficent deities with feelings of confidence, gratitude and, at most, affection; but not with love. This is psychologically comprehensible. For the natural polarity of fear is not love, but trust and security; thus it is these feelings which man in his fear wishes to recover and in which he wishes to dwell. The true antagonist of love is hate, not fear. The love of God corresponds to the hatred of Evil and the Devil.

Here we find ourselves in another order than that of fear and security. If we wish to idealize the situation, we may explain the hatred that incited the new fighters for Christ to acts of barbarism against paganism as a hatred of Evil. In truth, it was but the manifestation of unconverted barbarism intensifed by a vague desire to overcome a feeling of guilt, this latter stemming from the survival of paganism in the hearts of the champions of the new faith. However, the fundamental postulate of Christianity is the substitution for the old pair of opposites, "fear and security," the new polarity of "love and hate." Therefore we must ask ourselves whether our religion means more to us than mere security, or whether our love of God is sufficient to make us hate Evil.

To unite in one act and attitude the love and fear of God is a task as sublime as it is difficult. It almost transcends human capacity, yet it is the only one which fulfills God's reality. If today the intense experience of the fear of God may be said to be rare, this is because the love of God lacks immediacy. Under these circumstances, we can appreciate the wisdom of the Ten Commandments. They do not ask for the love of God. The existence of God is emphasized and demonstrated by a fact of history based on ethical postulates. "Thou shalt love God" belongs to a later period when that commandment could evoke a deeper understanding and a greater readiness than existed at Mount Sinai. Moreover, it is quesitonable whether the God of the Sinai revelation could be considered worthy of love. With good reason He did not reveal this aspect of His essence. What He asked for was gratitude and obedience for what He had accomplished, the exodus from Egypt. As He does not speak of His love for His people, so He does not ask it for himself. This is wisdom. There is not much sense in commanding love, for love cannot be enforced.

Here even God's omnipotence touches its limits. Man is asked to walk obediently in the ways of righteousness which the Decalogue discloses with incomparable clarity and beauty. The God of the Decalogue is obeyed, worshiped, and feared in the natural meaning of these words. The God of the New Testament is love. But God cannot be identified with love without the Christ's expiatory death and His essential identity with God. Only because of this identity can God be loved.

It is not difficult to understand how the God of the Old Testament evolves from a God who is feared to a God who is loved. It requires a greater effort to comprehend how the God of the New Testament, who is love, can be feared even in the sublime sense of veneration and awe. It was the difficulty in uniting these two aspects of God that tormented the medieval age; and I do not speak of the difficulty in reconciling the natural fear of God with the God of absolute love. This presents no theological

problem. To prove that absolute love may inspire veneration and awe does not at all facilitate the realization of
the experience of this love.

Compared with these crucial problems, the consideration of the diabolic appears refreshingly simple. Indeed,
what the Devil exacts is ever one and the same: the
hatred of God. In this respect, he is inexorable. The
hatred of God is the prerequisite of his own existence,
therefore his followers must share it. It is their pass-
word, the banner under which they march. Concerning
the sentiments of which he is the object, the Devil is
extremely modest, not to say indifferent. He does not ask
to be loved or feared. Only those fear the Devil who have
not surrendered to him. He who has given himself over
to the Devil lives henceforth in the satanic world as his
home; he has nothing more to fear, since he has accepted
the Devil's conditions. In this respect, the situation is the
exact reverse of that which prevails with God. He who is
with God fears Him, since fear, no less than love, is the
constituent of God's sphere. He who has lost the fear of
God is already half separated from Him, unless he is a
saint who participates in the pure love of God through
his mystic intuition. On the other hand, the Devil's
disciple is liberated from fear. Fear may return when the
term of the pact is concluded and the price must be paid.
But this is a psychological question and has nothing to
do with the fundamental relationship to the Devil. The
Devil requires from his followers neither fear nor love.
Loyalty is all he demands. Indeed, he can be compared
to a great feudal lord who in exchange for the benefits he
bestows on his followers requires faithful adherence to
his person and fidelity to the obligations contained in
the implicit or explicit pact. Such is his legitimate title.

In the sphere of the Devil, freedom from the fundamental feelings of fear and love simplify the inner life
and thus avoid many conflicts and problems. This seems

to many a desirable state. But such a path, once chosen, easily yet imperceptibly leads to a general loss of capacity for emotions and thereby runs parallel to, if not right into, the Devil's domain. For the Devil is distinguished by absolute emotional frigidity. Just as he does not ask for love or fear, he is himself free from these emotions. Indeed, he is free from all emotions except hate and its sadistic derivatives, such as cruelty and insidiousness.

Francisco Goya (1746-1828), *WHAT MORE IS THERE TO DO?*
from *THE DISASTERS OF WAR*

XII

THE DEVIL AND HISTORY

1

The Devil's philosophy of history is simple. His thesis is that the history of mankind is *his* history since the fall of Adam and Eve. This interpretation, he will insist (not without irony), is not his own invention but represents the decision of God himself.

The Devil's argument is, indeed, irrefutable. For he can quote God's own words spoken to Adam, first in the warning (Gen. 2:17): ". . . for in the day that thou eatest thereof [of the Tree of the Knowledge of Good and Evil] thou shalt surely die"; and second, after the Fall at the explusion from Paradise (Gen. 3:17): ". . . cursed is the ground for thy sake." There can be no misunderstanding of these fateful and terrible words. God's first enunciation severed Adam and Eve from the immortal beings to whom apparently they had been destined to belong and handed them over to destruction. The classic union of death and Devil here finds its first expression. In divesting Adam and Eve of their immortality, God surrendered them and their seed to the Devil. The cursed ground, that is, the earth, that now became the abode of Adam and Eve and of mankind is by definition the Devil's domain. As if this condemnation and damnation were not enough, God, having expressly cursed the serpent, promises (Gen. 3:15): "to put enmity between thee [the serpent] and the woman, and between thy seed and her seed," thus establishing a close tie, though of a negative character, between man and the Devil. With this three-fold curse, God set the monstrous pattern for the history of mankind.

The Devil has no reason to complain. He occupies the central position. He is right in feeling lawfully enthroned as lord of the world. We do not read anything into the texts which they do not contain. The apostle Paul (Col. 2:14) speaks authoritatively of "the bond which stood against us" (RSV), that is, of a debt imposed on mankind which mankind could not pay off and which was wiped out only by Christ's crucifixion. Proof of how seriously the Devil's claim to mankind as the seed of Adam has been taken can be found in the "lawsuits against the Devil," in which the Devil brings an action against God and Christ because Christ, against law and justice, disputes him his claim to mankind.

This claim was founded in original sin and expressly conceded to him by God—a favorite theme of theological jurists in the twelfth, thirteenth, and fourteenth centuries, when, after sagacious arguments produced by both sides, the Devil's case was dismissed on the ground that the expiatory death of Christ had wiped out mankind's sin. More than that: in the old Church, canonization was preceded by a kind of process in which the Devil's case was represented by a lawyer (*advocatus diaboli*) who raised objections to the canonization by quoting whatever could be said to the detriment of the candidate for sainthood. Similarly, in the old ritual of baptism the Devil was addressed in these words: "Harken, cursed Satan, I conjure thee by the name of the eternal God and our Lord Jesus Christ who has conquered thee with thy jealousy. . .," and his claim was rejected by these solemn words: ". . . I abjure thee, impure spirit, . . . retire from this servant of God. . . ." Nevertheless, it may be safely assumed, neither the

Devil's pretensions nor his self-pride were undermined by these attacks and defensive measures. The Devil still considers himself the lord of mankind and the source of its history, and he bases his claim on nothing less than the Holy Scriptures. There is even an argument that the sacrifice of the New Testament did not fundamentally change the situation.

The history of mankind goes back to an act of revolt and disobedience. Without Lucifer's revolt there would be no history, for it was he who seduced Eve to violate God's command. It is not only logical but imperative to assume that by seducing Eve Lucifer wanted revenge against God for his Fall; Eve's Fall, then, is the direct result of Lucifer's. It is small consolation for us that he thwarted God's designs, for with Eve's Fall he forced his entrance into the world of men. On the other hand, it is not edifying to imagine what would have happened without his interference. Since there is no indication of what God had planned to do with our ancestors, we can assume that He would have kept them forever as pets in the golden cage of Paradise. This is not a glorious prospect and most of us will prefer what actually happened, despite the price we have paid for our liberation.

Lucifer, indeed, lived up to the situation. True, he had not created Adam and Eve, but he took possession of them and out of innocent vegetating creatures made fully conscious beings possessing freedom and will. So, although he had not created our progenitors, he made them men and started the world drama as the fight between himself and God—no small achievement, whatever the outcome.

We shall return later to the utterly strange, even bizarre, fact that God was not obeyed either in the world of angels or by the first men. Both events, Lucifer's revolt and Adam's and Eve's disobedience, happened before history, in mythical time. This is why they did not happen once, or more than once, but as in the nature of the myth happen continuously. This also is why the question of truth or falsity does not reach them. Lucifer did not immediately make history. He had to wait for God to create the world and Adam and Eve. Then came Lucifer's opportunity. Using, or misusing, men's free will, he transformed them into finite beings and so created history. It was not an encouraging beginning. In the shadow of two supernatural acts of revenge, man begins his pilgrimage.

The human race and its history were born between revolt and revenge. Of justice, let alone love, there was no sign. The expulsion from Paradise was more than a punishment, it was the revengeful act of an infuriated God fearing for his privileges, as He openly stated (Gen. 3:22-23): "And the Lord God said: 'Behold the man is become one of us, to know good and evil; and now, lest he put forth his hand, and take also of the Tree of Life, and eat, and live forever. Therefore the Lord God sent him forth from the Garden of Eden. . . . " This certainly was worse than what Lucifer had done. The enormity of the punishment was out of proportion to the infringement. And so the history of mankind began with its greatest scandal, the expulsion from Paradise.

Shortly afterward man's dissension flared once again in the dramatic episode of Cain and Abel. In a strange but unmistakable form, it constitutes the continuation and consummation of the story of the Fall. The occasion is God's "respect" for Abel's offering of the firstlings of his flock and his lack of respect for Cain's offering of the fruit of the earth (Gen. 4:2). The Lord's preference for Abel, the keeper of flocks, for which no reason, not even a hint, is given, results in the slaying by Cain of his brother.

It is a strange and impenetrable story, but not entirely without a precedent. God's unprovoked and rather disdainful affront to Cain corresponds to the unprovoked temptation of Eve by the serpent. One cannot help feeling that in both cases snares were prepared to entangle the victims in their all-too-natural reactions. In the case of Cain, God seems to have recognized that His action in preferring Abel had been a mistake, and His punishment of Cain not only "set a sign for Cain, lest anyone finding him should smite him" (Gen. 4:15), but immediately after, and without any explanatory comment, we hear of Cain dwelling in the land of Nod, on the east of Eden, and building there a city.

Without unduly forgetting Lucifer's role, we can say that we owe to Eve and to Cain the fact *that* we are and *what* we are. Without Eve's decision to transgress God's commandment, our ancestors in all probability still would walk in the Garden of Eden clad in their innocence and in a state of moderate boredom (as is made plain by Eve's readiness to surrender to the first bit of something sensational). And had not Cain killed his brother, we still might be nomadic herders. It was Cain the city builder, and his immediate descendants, who invented the tent, musical instruments, and tools to cut brass and iron (Gen. 4:20). So to Eve we owe not only existence but our autonomy as creatures. To Cain we owe the foundations of civilization. And to both of them we owe freedom and progress, whatever they are worth.

Compared to Eve and Cain, Adam and Abel cut poor and pitiful figures. Adam's is a secondhand existence; he apparently lacks a will of his own. Abel is, like Adam, a good and innocent man without initiative or creative spirit. Both are left behind by mankind on its way. So the equation stands: Eve is to Adam as Cain is to Abel. Eve and Cain take their fate in their own hands. They are the first autonomous subjects and driving forces of history. Bernard Shaw, in his introduction to *Back to Methuselah*, sensed the situation. He wrote of a controversy between Adam and Cain in which Adam tried in vain to impose his authority. Having exhausted all arguments, he cited the ontological one: "After all I am the first man!" Cain remained unimpressed and retorted: "Being the first man is like being the first cabbage. I am the first murderer!" Indeed, Adam's only deed was that he permitted himself to be seduced. Eve made a decision and took the risk. She had no guarantees. She made history.

If social organization had developed according to merit, the Jews would have adopted the matriarchal system. But they did not. However, historical truth has been served by Cain's recognition as the primordial leader of mankind. Cain, whose spiritual ancestor was Lucifer, was not satisfied with the status of a created being; he asserted his rights and rose in protest against what he considered a flagrant injustice, even not shrinking from murder. It seems that God, though in His first reaction He cursed and outlawed Cain, upon reflection almost condoned the crime. However that may be, Cain is the true father of mankind, for with him man makes himself the master of his fate. Cain, indeed, ranks in stature with Prometheus. True, Prometheus was moved by compassion for miserable mankind when he acted against the will of Zeus and taught men the use of fire, and Cain cannot be called a philanthropist. But although Cain lacked the deeply humanitarian motive of Prometheus, he equaled his titanic boldness and independence, and the beneficent result of his action was no less substantial than that of Prometheus.

Both figures had this in common: they took a guilt upon themselves and through this guilt they became free (though guilt in each case does not carry exactly the same meaning). Prometheus offended the tyrant Zeus, who wanted to maintain mankind in its pitiful state of submission. Cain offended God by killing his brother, but succeeded in turning his punishment into a boon for himself and mankind. Both, in their struggle with the Godhead and through their suffering, transcended themselves and won freedom for their own and mankind's enrichment.

Between the condition of the relative innocence of Abel (for the absolute innocence of Paradise had been lost forever) and the state and process of civilization initiated by the guilt of Cain, we pursue our journey. The myth retains its truth. That does not mean that it is historically true, or a strange invention of the religious or philosophical mind; it means that it is born and lives on with mankind. The serpent of Paradise continues to tempt us with the same success it achieved with Eve; Adam and Eve are continually losing Paradise; the slaying of Abel goes on and Cain's creation and shaping of civilization continues. Such is the reality and truth of the myth.

2

The Devil succeeded in maneuvering man out of the state of innocence into the endless process of civilization. But this triumph holds even greater significance. Thanks to his effort, men no longer think of the state of innocence as enviable, nor do they show any desire to return to it. We look at innocence as a specific condition that, when applied in moderate doses, may be an antidote for certain conditions of civilization. But few see it as a dream. Innocence has fallen into such discredit that it has become the object of pity and contempt. Angelic purity and innocent naïveté find little comprehension or appreciation. There is no great figure less relevant to our time than St. Francis. Not that the men of his time were better than those of today. But their orientation and interest were not so unambiguously predestined as ours are; and saintliness is no longer a focus of understanding and appreciation. Also, what then fell to individual pity and love is now the task of social-welfare organizations of various kinds. Indeed, humanitarianism has increased together with the consciousness of responsibility, both perhaps corresponding to a growing incapacity to bear suffering, our own as well as that of others. Perhaps men are never asked to do the impossible but only as much as they can bear. Thus, asceticism is not lacking at present, it simply appears in other forms.

These forms, however, are no less cruel and inexorable than those of bygone epochs. There is the wild race for the imagined but dubious virtues of human life purchased at the price of a brief life-span, shaken health, and the renunciation of genuine enjoyment and knowledge. This is prodigious naïveté (or ignorance), but naïveté without innocence. Innocence in all its forms is disdained, whether it be virginal innocence or that of the saint. It is no longer considered something positive in its own right. What is valued is the absence of something undesirable, not the immediate presence of a positive state or quality. We admire the absence of corruption in politics and business, but few of us appreciate its opposite, innocence. The reason is that corruption is so rampant the vital issue is whether it is present or not, implying that its absence is so much a boon we do not look for more. Such is the general background against which the blindness to innocence must be seen and understood. Innocence in the original and positive sense of the term has no place in civilization; it has been supplanted by virtues such as decency, honesty, fair play—all of which, though praiseworthy and noble, belong to another category of human values.

Innocence is a state that precedes civilization. It existed in Paradise and therefore is a supernatural virtue recognized as such by medieval theology. It fell to man by an act of divine grace, and even among the saints of the Church few could lay claim to it. However, it served as a standard. In our times, the conditions for the application of this standard have failed. The belief in an indelible character, whether of a supernatural origin or not, runs against our deepest convictions and experience, and contradicts the evolutionary process of history. History succeeds and evolves against the background of paradisiacal innocence. From time to time, the fanatical longing for the lost Paradise flares up in theories and revolutionary movements that stigmatize the actual state of things. For example, the entire history of mankind as expressions of aberration or crime has been described by Rousseau and Karl Marx. Such views of history are rooted in a mixture of righteous feelings and utopian thinking. The Devil may have his hand in history, but he certainly cannot be held responsible for these all-too-human principles.

There is in this romantic conception of history (which is consciously or unconsciously influenced by biblical authority) so much confusion that a clarification of ideas becomes indispensable. This clarification centers on a new interpretation of the applicability of the terms "innocence" and "guilt" to man and to the history of man: it seems that a grave error, not to say crime, has been committed in applying these terms indiscriminately to man and his human condition whether inside or outside of Paradise. Concerning the situation in Paradise, the question is perfectly clear: before the Fall, absolute innocence, after the Fall, guilt. In other words, the very essence, the *ratio essendi*, of Paradise was innocence; therefore, its violation was guilt. Not so after Adam and Eve had left Paradise and entered the cursed soil of the earth. By eating the forbidden fruit, Adam and Eve had placed themselves under the sovereignty of

another pair of opposites: Good and Evil, which are by
no means identical with innocence and guilt.

The difference is evident. Innocence and guilt belong
to the criminal code. Adam and Eve, having violated the
statutes of the criminal code reigning in Paradise, expiated their crime by their expulsion from Paradise. The
prehistorical drama was terminated and the great mi-
gration through time and space, called history, began.
The period of innocence and guilt was finally left behind
and the rule of Good and Evil began. Moral order was
born. The Church has erred disastrously and fatefully in
ignoring, in essence as well as in time, this clear distinction. In permitting crime and guilt to merge with the
moral order and so to be carried with the latter into
history, the Church has charged mankind with an unbearable burden, the eternalization of original sin and
the necessity of atonement. It must be recognized that
the rule of innocence and guilt ended the moment Adam
and Eve set their feet on the soil outside of Paradise.

It is therefore just as meaningless to long for the
innocence of Paradise as it is superfluous to suffer from
the feeling of guilt. These categories belong to prehistory. In contrast to our temporal history, in which the
distinction between history and prehistory is uncertain
and vague, the moment in our spiritual history when we
cross from mythical into historical existence—that is,
the expulsion from Paradise—is unequivocally determined. From that time, men lived with Good and Evil;
innocence and guilt, in the metaphysical and religious
sense, lost their grip and meaning.

In the sphere of Good and Evil, called civilization,
what is the Devil's role and what are his designs? No
doubt the Devil has played a decisive role in creating
history. Causing the first man to break away from the
state of innocence was not intended to be an aim in
itself; it was the potential that this event created that

interested the Devil. Did he plan to establish an empire of his own by multiplying mankind? Did he simply want to obstruct God's intentions with regard to mankind, intentions of which we know nothing? And what were his specific ideas of interfering with and directing the ways of men? In their helplessness and disorientation, men have accused every terrestrial power, particularly the state, as being the Devil's work. The Church itself did not escape this suspicion—propagation was stigmatized; and in our time, communism is considered to be of infernal origin. Such are the main objects of the opprobrium. But leaving aside these more specific questions, let us return to the fundamental problem: What were the Devil's motives in creating, or at least in decisively interfering with, the history of mankind?

Two closely related possibilities stand out. First, the Devil wanted to obstruct God's intentions with regard to Adam and Eve. Second, he wished to create an empire of his own or enlarge the existing one, and since he could not hope to win new adherents among the angels exceeding the number of those who might have joined him in his rebellion, he saw Adam and Eve as a possible source of such strength.

As for the first possibility, it is particularly difficult to form an opinion, since the intentions of God with regard to Adam and Eve are entirely unknown. Were Adam and Eve to remain forever in the original state of absolute innocence? In view of the fact that they apparently possessed sex organs (since after the sinful act of eating the forbidden fruit their first reaction was to cover their nakedness, which can only mean their sex organs), it is unlikely. The difference between man and woman even in Paradise could not have made sense without corresponding physiological expression. If so, we must assume that God somehow planned the sexual union and propagation, for the aesthetic value of the sex organs as

merely decorative ornaments cannot be seriously de-
fended. Their prospective practical use was all the more
likely since all their other organs were functional. Thus
it was logical, and imperative, that sooner or later they
would make use of their sex organs too. But God evidently reserved the right to determine the time and
conditions of this fateful event. And here, no doubt, the
Devil intervened in thwarting once and for all God's
intentions with regard to mankind. We can assume, I
think, that we have been cheated out of our true destiny;
that we have bartered a wholly ambiguous life for a
glorious fate. In any case, the Devil triumphed and we
paid the price. It is up to us to see what we can make of
this intricate situation.

The Devil played God a nasty trick. Even more, he
succeeded in creating for himself a potentially inexhaustible reservoir, the unending stream of human lives
from which he could expect to siphon a predictable
number of victims to constitute his bodyguard and
retinue. Here we touch the principle of the Devil's philosophy of history. History must be a process without an
end. Any limitation in time would mean a limitation of
the number of followers. This view of history stands in
opposition to all traditional Western philosophy of history, which sees in history a meaning and aim to be
fulfilled within a limited time. More particularly, it
stands in opposition to the Christian philosophy of
history, which declares that history will end with the
return of the Savior. Christian, and all Western, philosophy of history views the historical process as happening
only once and within temporal limits, consciously or
unconsciously inspired by the idea that an endless historical process, or the endless repetition of the same
process, would annihilate the unique value of the human
individual and of the assumed meaning and aim of
history. The Devil is an individualist, but not in the

sense that he attributes a particular value to personality as such, and to its perfectibility. He is interested in isolating the individual and estranging him from God to incorporate him into his realm. In this sense, he apes sardonically God's appreciation of the infinite value of each individual human soul. On the other hand, it would be unjust to accuse the Devil of desiring mere quantity. He has, of course, his own standard of values. However, it remains true that the historical process for him serves the one and only purpose of gathering as many souls as possible into his sphere. For this reason history, for the Devil, must be limitless.

CITIPATI (DANCING SKELETONS)
Tibet, 17th century. This happy pair with legs interlaced dance upon a sea of blood, holding in their well-filled skull caps the blazing fire of wisdom which consumes evil in the unity of duality, merging the finite with the infinite.

XIII

THE DEVIL AND INFINITY

The Devil is godfather to mankind. But neither he nor God are particularly interested in the events of our history, or the evolutionary process we call history. Both God and the Devil have a simpler relation to history than we ourselves have. They look at the history of mankind less as an evolving drama comprising a variety of races, nations, and civilizations than as the sum total of individual men and their fate in this life and, traditionally, in their potential fate in the hereafter. The religious philosophy of history moves between the birth of the Savior and His return, the day of Last Judgment. And the Devil is concerned with history as a means of adding as many souls as possible to the infernal population.

The import of a world history in which God and the Devil combat each other for the possession of souls is double-edged. The religious philosophy of history exalts the value and dignity of man, but at the same time imposes upon him an almost unbearable burden and responsibility. The secular philosophy of history, however, stands on an entirely different ground. Whatever its concrete forms may be, they are all shaped by the conviction that the meaning of the historical process consists in the realization of an idea that is inherent in the process itself. The endless progress of civilization;

the interpretation put on mankind as a whole or on its
branches as an organism or a plurality of organisms,
and the ensuing picture of civilizations which rise,
flourish, and die according to a demonstrable law; the
metaphysical idea of the world spirit achieving ever-
growing self-knowledge through the historical process;
the exclusive significance of history in its function of
producing the great individual, the superman—these and
all other forms of the secular philosophy of history are
shaped by an idea that is one with history and inseparable from it.

On the contrary, seen from the viewpoint of God and,
even more so, of the Devil, the spectacle offered by
history, with all its apparent magnificence and perplex-
ing turmoil, has meaning and dignity only when it is
understood as the great battlefield where God and the
Devil fight for the souls of men. It is evident that the
divine and the diabolical intentions with regard to man's
eternal fate are not inherent in the process of history, as
are the constitutive principles of the secular philosophy
of history. They, rather, impart to history a purpose
remaining outside the march of history and untouched
by its vicissitudes. True, God, after Judaism in the
Western world, is likely to prefer a Christian civilization
to any other, yet even there His interest is not in the
civilization as such but in the number of pious men and
particularly of saints it produces. As for the Devil, we
may leave open the question of whether or not he ever
has succeeded in creating a satanic civilization; it is
enough to recognize that under various circumstances
he always has been able to recruit converts. Of course,
the Devil is more than just a kidnaper of souls. He is a
great stage manager with an acute sense of the dramatic
and the spectacular. We may well feel his hand in quite a
few scenes of the play called the History of Mankind and
at the same time be sure that he staged them in the first

place for his private amusement. Such interference with history, however, is to him nothing more than a pastime which does not impair but, rather, confirms the derisive view he holds of history—a view which boils down to the opportunity of seducing souls.

One reason why God and the Devil reject the views of the secular philosophy of history lies in the fact that it seems to preclude freedom of will. Indeed, predetermination of the march of history and its aims *must* limit the freedom of the individual will. If peoples and nations are agents and pawns in the hands of a predestined plan, it is difficult to see how the free will of the individual can be reconciled with the general conception of a preordained plan. One might theorize that the individual is free to act as he likes but that however he may act he finally will serve the preestablished purpose. But neither God nor the Devil would engage in so subtle a scheme. In their uncomplicated view of history, man remains the master of his fate. Any other view would contradict their essence.

Today a pragmatic and operational attitude has deprived the problem of freedom of will of the interest and esteem it once enjoyed in classical philosophy. The same observation applies to the philosophy of history. With the increasing interest in history, the desire to learn from the past by comparing its record with contemporary preoccupations has asserted itself. But beyond that, the need for a theoretical construction of the whole process of history is much less felt, and the question of the meaning and purpose of history does not greatly trouble the minds of men.*

We can see one reason for this change of attitude in the awareness that if ever there was an epoch that made

---

*The investigations of some Marxist revisionist philosophers in our time are an exception.

history it is ours. What there is of historical knowledge and theory almost immediately is absorbed by the effort better to understand and direct the manifold forces that melt into contemporary history and to foresee or control the results. This is not a time for disinterested and dispassionate reflection and abstraction which can engender a philosophy of history. It is not accidental that the last secular philosophy of history, that of Spengler, which looks at the great civilizations as organisms secluded within themselves and inacessible to each other's comprehension, signifies the end of the secular philosophy of history. And is equally significant that Toynbee's conception, with all its sovereign handling of historical material, ends in a religious philosophy of history. Nothing could better illustrate the fact that the secular philosophy of history has abdicated its role than these two examples so different in nature, yet so identical in meaning. The all-embracing and unifying power residing in theoretical consciousness has been appropriated by deliberate political will, although neither the means to achieve the end nor the end itself have assumed final shape.

Concerning the making of history in such dimensions as it is being made today, the secular philosophy of history is silent. The intended aim seems to be a kind of unified world in which all members cooperate and everyone has equal opportunities, rights, and duties. To realize this ideal, the first step is the amelioration of the situation in the backward and so-called underprivileged areas of the world and the creation of living conditions corresponding to the idea of the dignity of man. Thus, putting aside the philosophy of history with its belief in an inherent meaning and aim of the historical process, we take our fate in our own hands, freely determining what should be achieved and by what means. In assuming this pragmatic attitude, we take the same stand in relation to history as do God and the Devil. Both are indifferent to any inherent significance of history and judge it entirely from the viewpoint of their own interests and intentions. The resemblance of our attitude to that of the Devil is particularly striking. God (or the universe) may be held to be neutral or indifferent to human misery. We even may say that He shows a certain predilection for this indifference because of its twofold function of serving as a trial and test and of offering through love and mercy the opportunity to act. The Devil as well has no interest in human misery, nor in grace and compassion, not only because he necessarily antagonizes God but also because wealth and power carry greater temptations than humility and suffering.

More important, misery tends to dehumanize man and endanger his existence and his being. All this is against the interest and designs of the Devil, for—as the Arab saying has it—"the Devil does not destroy his own house." Thus in our pragmatic attitude to history, and in our opposition to misery, we find the Devil our ally.

This unexpected alliance has even deeper common roots. God's world of men is limited in time. It begins with the creation of the world and the creation of the first man. It will end with the return of the Savior. In the view of modern science, the age of the earth can be determined, and if its end (coinciding perhaps with the destruction of the solar system or the disappearance of the atmosphere*) cannot be computed with the same precision, both events are to our standard so remote that the time of their happening equals infinity. However, in our modern world picture, the earth disappears in the universe, and it is the universe that sets the measure and the catagories for our thinking. There the concep-

---

*Ecological, and genetic factors, as well as demographic ones, including the possibility of a nuclear holocaust, also must be considered.

tions of beginning and end lose their meaning and are superseded by the idea of the infinite and an ever-expanding cosmos. So, in the conception of the extension of the universe as well as of its smallest particles, the idea of the infinite must be introduced and redefined.

The Devil's world picture resembles ours. True, he must unwillingly acknowledge that the world is God's creation, but everything in him rebels against its coming to an end in a predictable future time. His interest requires a perpetual world. We do not know whether he possesses the means to interfere with God's intentions, as he did so successfully at the world's beginnings, but we may be sure that he strives for perpetuity in order to increase the dimension of his sphere. The idea of the infinite and the boundless rules our thinking and determines our outlook on life, fate, and actions; and this opens a road to the Devil. It does not inevitably lead to him, but it certainly forms a potential link with him.

All great historical periods have had their particular relation to the Devil. In the Middle Ages, the experience of and the emphasis on sin kept the Devil constantly within the range of vision; at other times, frenetic sensuality and worldliness invited his approach; or lust for power in any of its forms attracted him. Today the conditions that in the past made sin the most formidable of moral categories and the supreme concern of man do not exist any more; frenetic sensuality often lives more in the imagination than in reality; and worldliness has become so natural and sophisticated that it cannot seriously be connected with the Devil. It is quite different, however, with the lust for power. Ever present in some form or other, it has today freed itself from the fetters that tempered it in the past. It is no longer restricted to specific fields such as politics or religion but has assumed almost absolute authority, determining the atmosphere and motives of action.

In the nineteenth century it was the general belief that there were limits set to our knowledge, experience, and power. During the last few decades these limits have been shifted so far beyond their former position that it has become difficult to perceive them at all. To the conception of infinite space, whatever be the definition of infinity, corresponds the will combined with the technical possibility to conquer the universe. For the earth has become too small. The idea of leaving the earth and advancing into outer space comes not only from the scientific mind and a lust for adventure but also from technical and military considerations. It seems almost paradoxical that space and time had to be conceived as infinite and the concept of the infinite introduced into mathematics to form an idea of the extension of the universe, the age of its constituent parts, and to make predictions about its future. Springing from these theoretical achievements, appliances carry men or missiles which, with every-increasing velocity, conquer space and time. And the conquest of space and time parallels another endeavor, the prolongation of the life-span of man. Logically, this is the first step to the conquest of death and to the existence of eternal youth, the subject of so many myths and legends. The successful fight against some diseases and the demonstrable prolongation of the average life-span are only the first steps along a road the course and end of which cannot be foretold. If conquest of space and time, and victory over disease and death are our motives and aims, it is safe to predict that it is an effort without end. And, after all, what will have changed once we travel with vertiginous velocity to the planet Mars or Venus and succeed in living to the 969 years of Methuselah? These and similar achievements may seem to us today the peak of triumph and happiness. But actually nothing will have been changed; the same desires and temptations, in slightly new disguise, will take the place of the old ones. The objective attained no longer satisifes our desire. Everything becomes preliminary and preparatory to a still further goal. The way, and not the station reached, fascinates and captivates our imagination. Thus we are doomed to overlook the fact that the stations essentially resemble each other. The proportions remain the same, only the dimensions and magnitudes are different. It is not that the objectives are wrong, illusory, or unworthy, but that their acceptance as the only, or the supreme, objective is fallacious.

The conquest of space and time and the extension of life cannot be the end. On the contrary, it is the means to an end, concerning the nature of which there can be no doubt. It is the eradiction of fear and anxiety and their replacement by that which is unqualified and conclusive. If this is so, we move in a circle. For the fulfillment can only lie at infinity. What we really need and search for is a central and positive aim of existence to which the conquest of space and time and the extension of life become subordinate. The astonishing fact is not that we are attracted by the infinite but that we can enter into a positive relation with it. We can think the infinite, handle the infinite in our thinking, and act in the direction of the infinite, but we cannot be infinite, at least so long as we live on earth.

Here lies our limitation, to which we are bound to submit. It is enough—indeed, it borders on the miraculous—that we as finite beings are able to maintain a positive and creative relation with the infinite. It follows, however, that the infinite cannot be allowed to dominate our minds. This is not to depreciate the infinite or the manifold endeavors which take the conception of the infinite as their base. Rather, we emphasize the need to determine the place the infinite must take in our existence—a measure of self-protection that prevents the superhuman from exerting a dehumanizing influence. For this purpose, an image and idea of man are needed which our epoch so far has not been able to produce. If we fail in this task, the overemphasis on the infinite will in the long run have a negative effect on man's life and work. Unconditional orientation to the infinite and permanent preoccupation with the preparation for the future and the expectation from the future of fulfillment and happiness must eat away what is best in man.

Apparently our epoch shares with the Devil the interest in extensive infinity, at least so far as the infinity of time is concerned. True, the bases of this interest differ: the Devil needs infinite time to fill his realm with human souls; man seeks it to increase his knowledge and power and to prolong his life-span. But without knowing it, man through his attitude conjures up the Devil. The critical point lies in the fact that man, by surrendering to extensive infinity, imperils the core of his being, which is finite and demands limitation and measure. The flight into infinity breeds vain ambition, disappointment, and disintegration—conditions which permit easy entrance for the power of Evil under manifold disguises. Lacking a center and shorn of a formative principle, man seeks to fill his life with gifts and promises, the granting of which is the Devil's prerogative.

AMITAYUS, BUDDHA OF INFINITE LIFE AND IMMORTALITY
Tibet, 18th century. The Buddha sits in meditative repose holding a vase
containing the water of immortality. He is invoked in rites for healing evil
forces, prolonging life-power, paralleling the Christian Eucharist.

XIV

THE DEVIL AND IMMORTALITY

The Devil before his fall had no relation to time. True, like all the angels, he had a beginning because he had been created by God. But this must not tempt us into introducing time categories of "before and after" which have no place in the celestial world. For God *is*. He is absolute, and identical with pure being. He has no relation to time; indeed, speaking figuratively, we might think of Him as pure presence. Therefore the angels, though created, have been created as eternal beings, which means that their way of being and thinking cannot be covered by our conception of the boundless and the infinite (which are merely negative characteristics and cannot convey an idea of the positive reality).

As for Lucifer, we can assume that, through his fall and particularly through his decisive interference with man's fate, he separated himself from heavenly timelessness and plunged headlong into the world of the finite and the relative. Such change, however, cannot mean that he ceased to exist as a timeless being. Since the Devil chose to act in the world of men, he had to adjust himself to it; this meant thinking in terms of finiteness while remembering celestial infinity. It is certainly not more difficult to imagine an eternal being descending into our finite world than to believe that creatures limited and finite are called to eternal life. And did not

God Himself, as the Christ, appear on earth and even assume human shape in order to deliver mankind from the powers of Evil?

Thus we can imagine Lucifer firmly established in our world and here pursuing his aims. But at the same time we can think of him as the great angel of the celestial hierarchy who, though damned and banished from the presence of God, continues to enjoy the timeless eternity of heaven. In his relation to our world, Lucifer, now the Devil, has to accept its idea of infinity equaling endless duration as opposed to finiteness and impermanence. As an eternal being, he is beyond this pair of opposites. Therefore he is not in opposition to finiteness but without any relation to it.

This two fold aspect confers on the Devil, a divided and strangely fascinating character. On the one hand, he is deeply involved in the affairs of this world, at home in its remotest corners, versed in all its tricks, in intimate contact with men and intensely interested in their behavior, more so even than God. On the other hand, he looms as the dire power of Evil, inaccessible in his grandeur. He is the fiend. In the first, the secular, aspect he seems willing and able to grant the fulfillment of a desire so near to our hearts: the prolongation of life, if not indefinitely at least far beyond its present limits. This is proved by the black art of the Middle Ages. In his second aspect, the eternal angelic being, like God he can guarantee true immortality after death, an immortality that the Church, perhaps unjustly, has in the past depicted as eternal damnation in the torments of hellfire. The Church, of course, sees hell as a deterrent. But even the prospect of hell has failed to deter us from evildoing. For our fear of death, of complete annihilation, is so great, and the desire to survive is so deep-rooted, that the question of the "how," of the form of survival, is of secondary importance. In the face of complete obliteration anything seems better than nothingness.

The idea of turning to the Devil in search of immortality may cause some misgiving. It need not, however, once we decide to face realistically the situation of man. Born into conditions he could not master or undo; leading his life between manifest contingency and recognized necessity; searching for life's aims which become inscrutable as they deviate from his immediate needs; enduring the miseries of life for which he can be held responsible only to a modest degree—man may plead innocence and ignorance; but only blindness and arrogance can hide reality from him. He may well turn to God and say: "Who am I to aspire to immortality?" And his voice will be filled with deeper contrition or bitterness the more he thirsts for immortality, if only as a compensation for what he has suffered and missed in this life. He may rise in revolt and despair, but nothing will convince him that his situation entitles him to immortality. Yet there remains the desire to find immortality—and a power that promises to change radically our situation in this world, to raise us beyond its limitations here and hereafter, is attractive, if nothing else.

We also may ask: Who has the greater interest in human immortality, God or the Devil? For it is obvious that he who has the greater interest in immortality will do more to promote it. True, theologically speaking, God has created man, though for what reason and to what purpose remains unknown. There cannot be any doubt, however, that God is sufficient unto himself. Besides, He is surrounded by the host of His angels and He could continue to create any number of them. But the Devil is alone. With his boundless will to power and his insatiable thirst for revenge, he is eager to build his empire in the face of God. As long as he was the first of the angels he was self-sufficient; after the fall and his self-willed transformation, he was nowhere; he had to create a world for himself. So he recognized the potentialities hidden in the first man and secured a position from which he could not be dislodged. Thirst for revenge induced him to draw men over to his side and persuade them to make common cause with him.

A kind of mutual dependency has been established; but the scale of the balance weighs decidedly in favor of men. It is the Devil who is desperately in need of human satellites to populate his realm, for there is, as far as we know, no other reservoir on which he can draw. On the other hand, it is difficult to see what means, if any, we possess to exploit this promising position to our advantage. The Devil, of course, does everything to accommodate us with whatever we ask of him, but unfortunately, it looks as if whatever we receive from him never can outweigh what he demands from us. So, until a way is found to end this tragic situation, we cannot but make the best of it.

As for immortality, the desire of men seems to parallel that of the Devil. He is ready to help man in his effort to prolong life on earth. He is equally willing to guarantee perpetual life after death, under his own conditions, of course. Such promises seem to quell man's fear of death and annihilation. Here is a tie between man and Devil as strong as the granting of earthly possessions, perhaps even stronger. The relation to time which is the Devil's, since he is the fallen angel, corresponds to man's natural desire for permanence, here or in the hereafter.

This concept has nothing in common with the transcendence of time which God and whoever enters the heavenly kingdom enjoy. What reigns there is not endless time, nor permanence in time; it is *transcendence* of time as of space (for permanence and impermanence are inseparable). It is pure presence without any relation to past or future. But indisputable as this conclusion may be, there remains the difficulty emphasized above: God, being sufficient unto himself, is not in need of man and therefore has no intrinsic relation to man's immortality. We even may argue that not only is God not in need of man and his immortality but that the truly God-fearing man himself does not care about immortality. Indeed, the pious man who walks in the ways of righteousness finds reward and satisfaction in the knowledge that he fulfills God's commandments, in accordance with biblical instructions. To please God and to devote himself to God is his only desire. If God grants eternal life, he will gladly accept it; if life comes to an end on earth, it does not disturb him, for he has done all he could, and there cannot be greater satisfaction. This is the attitude at the root of the Old Testament's impressive silence on the question of immortality.

Concerning the Devil, the situation is simpler. The Devil is not self-sufficient, he needs ever more advocates and increasing power to have his revenge on God. His most valuable ally is man. Therefore, the man who surrenders to the Devil may be sure that he is well taken care of and that his immortality is guaranteed. True, the immortality granted by the Devil is of another kind than that bestowed by God. It does not transcend time; it is the endless continuation of the time lived here. God's gift of immortality leaves everything temporal behind; it is transformation and elevation to another plane distinguished by the absence of any relation to time. It is pure present, pure immediacy; it is peace in God. This pure present can be called infinity only metaphorically, and speaking of it as being eternal would be redundant. For a moment may be eternity itself and time but a figment of the imagination. There can be no peace *in* the Devil; at best there can be only peace *with* the Devil. However, the immortality promised by the Devil is certain to be granted; it also is more easily obtained and nearer to understanding. All this was duly felt and appreciated by the Middle Ages.

With our orientation to the infinity of time and space,

we are moving in dangerous proximity to the diabolic world. Science moves onward in a straight line, and all errors, deviations, and redefinition of principles are swept aside by the steady progress which achieves its aim at infinity. There hides the great temptation of unconditionally giving oneself over to the idea of endlessness. There lie not only the peril of seriously undermining a sound life but also a surrender that may produce consequences reaching beyond the borderline of reason.

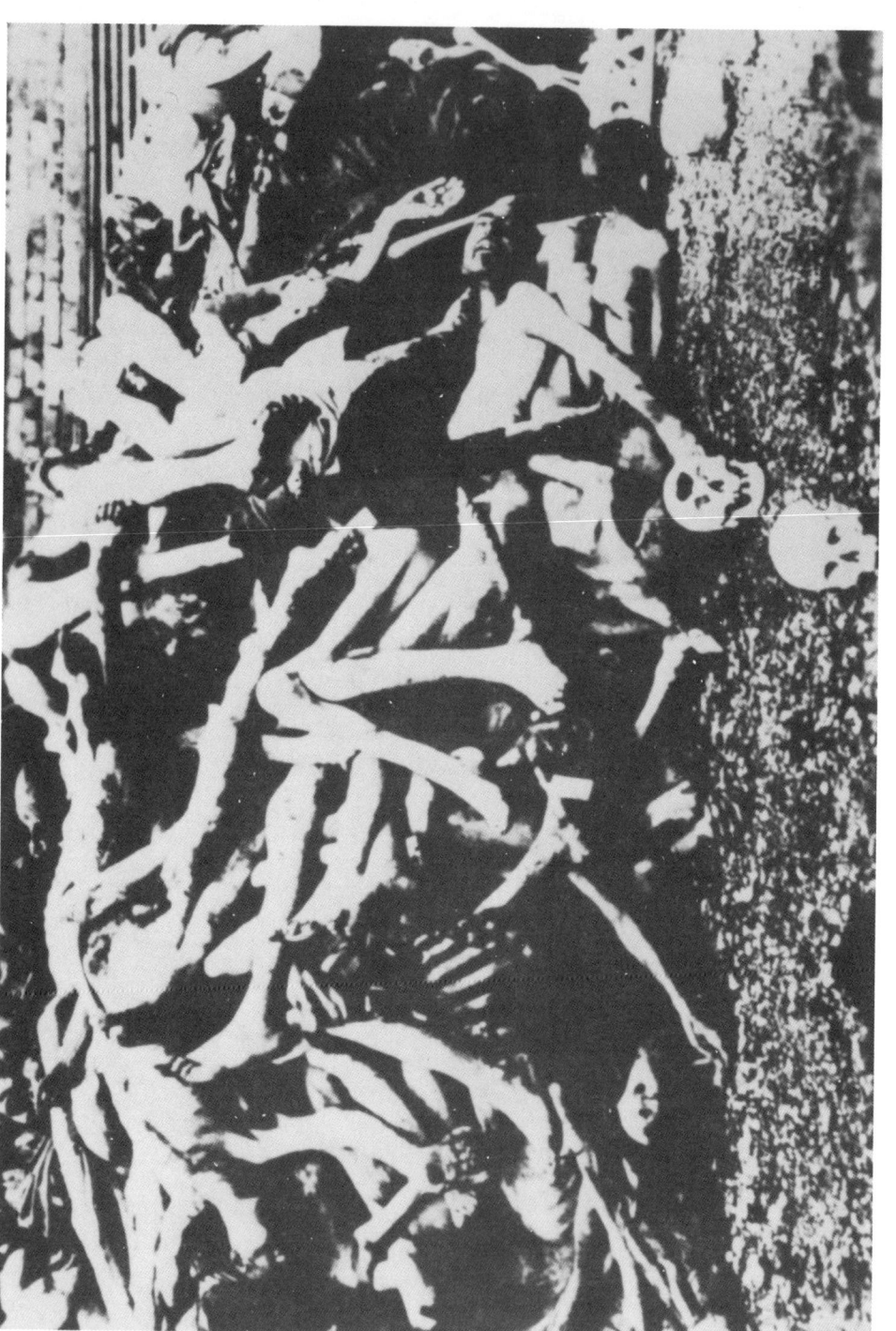

Charred bones of men, women and children, taken from the ovens in the Nazi Holocaust, (1945) Auschwitz, Germany

XV

THE PERSONIFICATION OF EVIL

It is a time-honored question whether God created man "in His image after His likeness" (Gen. 1:26) or vice versa. Xenophon said that "the Aethiopian imagines his gods black and flatnosed, the Thracian blond and blue-eyed; indeed, if the horses and oxen knew how to paint, the horses would represent their gods as horses, the oxen theirs as oxen." In both these views, different as they are, man holds a distinguished place. Man came last among God's creations; he was the highest achievement because God had made the world for him and for his use. And man, having no greater dignity to confer than his own likeness, could not do better than provide his humanlike gods with human attributes, but raised to a higher power. As for Xenophon's theory, however, it is unlikely that the anthropomorphic act was so immediate and precise. The humanlike image of God or the gods is a late product of the evolution of the mind.

Man's religious career does not appear to have started with the elevation of the form of the human person to a suprahuman realm. The fundamental experience was that of an irrational, impersonal power, called *mana* in anthropology, pervading all existence, though distributed unevenly among men as among objects. These accumulation centers of power—feared, awesome, conciliated, and handled for good as well as for evil purposes by the shaman or fetish-priest—constitute the momentous legacy of our ancestors from which the later forms of religion evolved. As the consciousness of the self and its endowment was clarified in man, he intuitively imposed his qualifications on other phenomena of nature, on living creatures or on the products of his imagination. And so arose the animistic world picture that over a long period dominated the beliefs of man and, even after its dethronement, continued to influence poetic and philosophical thought. Man began to feel that he stood out against animate and inanimate nature, perhaps even against the supernatural; and on this firm ground he could establish the foundations of science and scientific method, thereby bestowing on him a dangerous supremacy and independence.

It is difficult to call the God of the Old Testament an anthropomorphic God if we believe that He created man in His image. However, His greatness as it appears at Mount Sinai is considerably impaired by many of His actions and reactions—all too human and even inhuman —that are reported in the first five books of the Old Testament. Indeed, the God of the Ten Commandments speaks to men in the words of men. It is all the more surprising that this God, who speaks in the words of men and acts in the ways of men, should solemnly forbid the making of images, even an image of himself. Close as He is to Moses and the Jews, He is unwilling to make this trifling concession to human frailty. Indeed, what He did by stigmatizing any likeness made of himself represents the most momentous act in the history of religion and religious veneration in the West. He separated once and for all the idea of personality from its physical appearance and, in so doing, established the immaterial person, the spirit as personality, as the highest reality, even though He reserved this privilege for Himself and did not extend it to His human creatures.

The Old Testament remains stubbornly silent on this subject, the elucidation of which apparently would have reflected on the problem of immortality. However, it is to the eternal merit of the old Hebrews to have recognized in their idea of God the essentially immaterial nature of personality. It is not mere chance that this insight was reached in a Middle Eastern country. Nowhere as in the religions of the peoples dwelling in the lands from Egypt to Mesopotamia have the figures of the gods been thrown into such bold relief, their characters marked with so stern a dignity and their significance revealed through their deeds and adventures in heaven, on earth, and in the netherworld. All this is in striking contrast to the Greek deities, who are seen as all too human and frolicsome and as metaphorical appendages of philosophy and poetry. The Hebrews grasped the innermost significance of this pantheon and in a great intuitive leap hypostatized the idea of personality in the recognition of their own personal God, pure spirit without history and without beginning and end.

In the civilizations east of Mesopotamia, the act of personification does not reach into the highest sphere of religious reality. The two gods of Iranian dualism, Ahura Mazda and Angru Mainyu, are names given to the principles of Good and Evil, but they cannot be called genuine personifications, lacking as they do any individual life. In the Indian pantheon, teeming with personifications of all kinds, the personifying urge halts reverently before the ultimate reality, which defies any anthropomorphic interpretation. The same is true for China. Thus, at least with regard to the ultimate reality, the East rejected and transcended the anthropomorphic view while the West continued to adhere to it, substituting for its polytheistic anthropomorphism the great paragon of Hebrew monotheism in its Christian offspring.

So the West and the Middle East were linked by one of the momentous objectivations of history, that of the idea of personality and therefore also of history. However, it soon became obvious that the objectivation corresponding most deeply to the Western mind, and the one that the Western mind could truly call its own creation, was of another kind, one which formed the basis and goal of scientific thought. And this objectivation was inexorable in its claim to sovereign rule. The rise of the modern mind was accompanied by a consistent bent toward depersonalization, starting with the trend to replace the personal God by pantheistic conceptions. The Devil suffered the same fate and Evil began to claim the place occupied hitherto by Satan.

In an earlier chapter we discussed why the commonly accepted opposition of Good versus Evil is wholly inappropriate and misleading; that the genuine opposition is saintly versus Evil and good versus bad. As stated above, the saintly was contained in and grew from the *mana*, the magic stuff that was believed to be distributed (though unequally) among inanimate objects and animate beings, thus obliterating the distinction between the animate and the inanimate. In due course this irrational power became, so to speak, the raw material out of which the supernatural capacities of the deities were shaped, and it is above all the awe and veneration-inspiring quality of the saintly that best preserves the energy and character of its origin. The same applies in its own way to Evil. Therefore, in the strict philosophical sense, only saintly and Evil are true substances; Good and bad are merely derivatives. Good and bad refer only to persons, the essential nature of their intentions and actions, their improper use for designing the constructive or harmful. On the other hand, the saintly and the Evil point beyond the human sphere, which we may identify with the metaphysical or, according to our religious conviction, with the realms of God and the Devil.

Metaphysically the saint exists because there is the saintly; the evildoer exists because there is Evil. Religiously the saint exists because there is God, the sum and substance of the saintly; the evildoer exists because there is the Devil, the sum and substance of Evil. In the West there always has been a pronounced inclination to connect the recognition of the saintly and the Evil with their personifications. Correspondingly, when the personifications began to fail, the saintly and the Evil abdicated in favor of the Good and the bad. Such developments were concomitant with an impoverishment of the spirit of man and the idea of man. To live life within the limits of the moral categories "Good" and "bad" certainly makes life easier, but it does so at the price of man's dignity and greatness. For it is the saintly and the Evil which open the door to man's final self- realization and which permit him to transcend himself.

It may be difficult for our time to recognize that Good and bad are not the supreme values. They are not even independent values. Indeed, to know what they really are is the reflection of saintly and Evil. Only when we face transcendent goodness may we awaken to the consciousness of something extraordinary happening and be induced to speak of a saintly person without, however, realizing the revolutionary implication of our awareness. The Good and the bad can rule in their moral realms so long as they carefully avoid impinging upon the superior powers of the saintly and the Evil. Such an enounter might easily result in their being forced to recognize the suzerainty of the saintly and the Evil.

Today we prefer to remain on the level of Good and bad. Our reasons are as obvious as they are manifold. Common to them all is an aversion to the extreme and hazardous so far as man is concerned. In contrast to our

bold, even adventurous, spirit in science is our attitude
to ourselves and to our idea of man. In this respect we
have become increasingly indifferent, timid and easily
satisfied, preferring the average and the assurance offered by the concrete and practical. This is inevitable,
since the scientific mind, in contrast to its thrust in its
own field, tends to exert a leveling influence in all other
fields of thought. Under these circumstances, the sense
for the saintly and the Evil is on the point of being
obliterated. Even the concepts of Good and bad are
increasingly interpreted as being identical with the
socially useful or harmful. It is no wonder, then, that the
Devil has disappeared and that God himself has withdrawn to the periphery, visible in the far distance as the
abstract personification of the Good.

This does not mean that God and the Devil have
ceased to exert power and influence. They continue to
operate, but our indifference blinds us to their presence.
And the Devil more than God benefits by this state of
things, for he is accustomed to plot in darkness and to
act indirectly through delusion and temptation.

One well might ask here why the idea of personifying
"Good" and "Evil" could have arisen in the first place.
What kind of folly or madness could have induced man
to make his life miserable by raising two simple moral or
psychological phenomena to the rank of an intimidating
superhuman power? To answer, we must, in the light of
our argument, restate the question with greater precision: What has been and remains the incentive to personify the saintly or the divine? And what has been and
is the incentive to personify Evil? For, strange to say, the
respective incentives not only are not the same but are
diametrically opposed to each other. Evil is infinitely
more gruesome when it is thought of or experienced as
an impersonal power than when it is represented by the
figure of the Devil. Impersonal Evil, nonobjective Evil,

unseen and unidentifiable, lurks everywhere and its threat emerging from the dark makes hell of life. But when Evil is incarnated in the Devil, there is open confrontation; and though one is aware of the Devil's working (preferably in the dark), the certainty of dealing with a personal adversary confers on the encounter a comprehensible and human character otherwise absent. Moreover, seen from the viewpoint of the aspirant to Evil, the act of handing oneself over to impersonal Evil is but a lonely and gloomy prospect as compared with the encounter with the Devil, imagined or real, where the pros and cons are discussed with the great adversary himself and the terms are negotiated.

Even the mere idea and conviction that there is a personal power of Evil, without the medieval paraphernalia, involuntarily confers upon the moral and spiritual struggle a vivid and distinct character that facilitates decision.* Psychologically speaking, therefore, the personification of Evil derives from an intuitive act of self-defense to ward off the unbearable impact of anonymous Evil.

As for the motivation that led to the personification of the saintly (and therewith of the Good), this has its roots in opposite psychological conditions. The saintly is less impressive when it presents itself as isolated, as a mere disposition of the soul, than when it is seen against the background of God. Where Evil invites personification to become less oppressive and ghastly, the saintly seeks personification to find fulfillment and self-realization in God. There is no denying that the connection between the saintly and its divine personification is deeper and stronger than that between Evil and the Devil. However, our human experience suggests the inverse evaluation.

*See the German word for deep anxiety, *Angst*, which means anxiety but not directed to an object.

We feel that it is easier to be satisfied with the autonomous existence of the saintly than with that of Evil. Evil, provided we realize the the fullest extent what it means, is unbearable if it is not personified.

There is another, perhaps more striking, reason why the saintly invites personification. The saintly is simple, unassuming, sincere and, within certain limits, immutable. So is God eternally the same, and so He reveals Himself to His saints as the eternal light and infinite love. Yet He has no form: for if He had He might as well don another or a plurality of others, and such variability would be incompatible with the One God. The Devil, for example, does not appear in one shape only. Perhaps an immaterial and infinite being, when it chooses to appear in material form, cannot be satisfied with just one and the same aspect. However, in relation to the Devil, the variety of his disguises is almost without end. Not only does he assume such animal forms as the classic buck (he-goat), the sow, the gigantic toad, and many others, he may appear in such human form as a possessing, diabolic influence over other men; as a man of strange beauty; as a woman, a monk, or in any disguise the occasion may demand. He uses this art to seduce and to terrify. At the same time, he presents himself as the real lord of this world, disposing of what it contains at will and opening the doors to other unknown and attractive, though destructive, worlds.* This art of disguise imparts to the Devil that strange intermediary existence between being and nonbeing that we discussed earlier. However, it is his way of life: unrest and uncertainty; a way of life in which his satellites participate. He seems to be ubiquitous. His prerogative is to be everywhere at the same moment. He dons all shapes. But which is the

*Through the promiscuous use of psychedelic drugs, for example, which lead to apathy and the destruction of personality.

real one, and is there a real one?

All this is the opposite of God. In God there is peace, and His ubiquity is omnipresence without disguise. God *is*. He does not appear in any form and His voice at all times is the still, small, inner voice. The Devil appears in a confusing variety of forms, of which those reported in the Middle Ages are only the crudest manifestations. Metaphorically, he may be said to live in his whisperings and temptations and the fleeting images he conjures. The traditional relationship between the Devil and death reveals itself here too. In the allegorical dances of death, the subject of so many representations in art throughout the centuries, death, though inexorably the same, appears in all kinds of disguises according to the age, sex, and stage in the life of "its" victims. Devil and death are the two scourges and specters of mankind everywhere— ever the same, yet changing their manifestations.

Hans Baldung (ca. 1484-1545), *THE RAPE OF HELEN* "Whosoever lieth with a beast shall surely be put to death." Exodus 22:19.

XVI

THE DEVIL AND SEX

The God of the Old Testament is a masculine god in a man's world. In the New Testament He fulfills himself by sending to earth His only Son, out of compassion for humanity. The Christ is not a figure fitting the Old Testament, since the Christ or Messiah is still to come in history. He conquers the male principle in himself; the feminine principle does not triumph. Christ unites and transcends both male and female and leads man, the creature of God, to supremacy on earth. This is the meaning of the words He speaks at the marriage in Canaan: "Woman, what have I to do with thee?" He does not reject His mother but, rather, the feminine principle, which, even as the masculine, has left Him. He is beyond sex as God is Himself.

The difficulty in conceiving of a personal God as being sexless may constitute only an imagined problem; yet it persists. The East in its nonpersonal, nonhistorical conceptions abandoned the idea of personality as well as the monotheistic concept. It abrogated rational definitions and was content with indicative terms pointing to a state yet to be realized. We in the West cannot avoid the problem by speaking of God in the neuter gender, as *It*, since this would deprive Him of the character of personality. Even if we speak of God as the Supreme Being, we imply personality and therewith the masculine sex. However, though we cannot earnestly connect the idea of the one personal God with the attribution of sex, there is no denying the fact that our immediate feeling identifies God with the male. Nor can the problem be dismissed as purely grammatical or semantic, nor even reduced to the patriarchal nature of our society. When all this is said the fact remains that it is clearly impossible for us to think of God as female.*

Similarly, the great Adversary of God cannot be conceived as being anything but masculine. There is a deep reason for this. A female principle of Evil would necessarily appear more as a complement of God—who cannot be complemented. So the true opponent of God must be masculine. True, the Devil is essentially a nonincarnate being and so beyond sex. But as a result of the perversion of his nature, he becomes intimately connected with matter and the phenomenal world of men, with men's instincts, concupiscence, seemingly lofty desires, and ambition. These he tries to misguide and pervert, and to accomplish this aim, he must appear to be man's equal, accessible to his comprehension and aspirations. So he had to choose a sex, and for the above-stated reasons, it had to be male.

In this respect, the Devil does not present a problem. With the Devil, personality and sex are inseparably connected. Were he deprived of his masculine character, he would disappear into the impersonal state of Evil. The Devil, in view of his intentions on earth, cannot be thought of as sexless or beyond sex. On the contrary, his capacity for transformation permits him to appear in all

---

*This is strikingly illustrated by our instinctive reaction to the following historical anecdote. In the first days of the suffragette movement in England, Mrs. Emmeline Pankhurst and a young woman were imprisoned for demonstrating. Mrs. Pankhurst tried to console her companion with the words: "Now cheer up, my dear, and put your trust in God. *She* will not desert us."

kinds of disguises, male and female, but his true nature remains masculine. Hence his powerful relation to the feminine sex, starting with Eve, and the important role the woman plays in the diabolic world. However, there are no female devils. There are fanatic women satellites such as witches, but it is unlikely that women ever have held a high rank in the hierarchy of hell.

The Devil owes everything to woman. It was Eve who started the process of history, which was all the Devil wanted or needed. One would expect the Devil to show himself grateful by granting to woman the decisive role in human history. But no such thing happened. The Devil has an excellent memory, but gratitude is not one of his virtues. History has become man's history, determined by man for his own aims. Much is to be said for the idea that history might have taken a better turn if woman had been in charge of it. As it happened, the matriarchy was not more than a sporadic phenomenon in history; its influence was negligible. On the other hand, it can be said that woman has not fared too badly in the masculine world even though she has had to resort for the most part to indirect influence to achieve her aims. This, with only a few notable exceptions, has been her way to achieve greatness and power on the highest level of society and state, no less than in the more simple stations of life.

If we agree that to be led astray by the Devil is more justifiable and in some ways more honorable than to be led astray by one's wife, then Adam is left in a rather dubious position. Eve had been misguided, but she herself misguided Adam. There is a sound balance. Adam, on the contrary, was nothing but an object—a sad role, particularly for a man. This is why it must be emphasized that Eve and Cain are our ancestors in spirit and that we had better forget Adam.

The biblical origin of woman has no great dignity. God,

in creating woman from Adam's rib, denigrated, if not humiliated, her. The conclusions that can be drawn from this derivative origin are obvious, since it appears that God, had He so desired, could have given woman a material form from another source. As it was, her way of coming into existence must have lowered her self-respect as it inevitably denigrated her position in the eyes of Adam. It was as natural for her to grasp any opportunity of improving her station as it was for Lucifer to take advantage of the situation. Indeed, in turning to her instead of to Adam and in giving her the privilege of free decision, the Devil did what he could to build up her personality and self-respect. He permitted her as a human being to rise above Adam who, in reality, became her inferior and a kind of annex. But despite Eve's towering personality, her social status and authority continued to be subordinated to Adam's, and so it has remained. Why? And why did Lucifer not do anything to continue his work of liberation and secure for Eve and her offspring, if not a dominating, at least an equal, position to that of Adam and his sex?

There is only one possible answer. Lucifer, after all, was masculine. He went as far as he could go, but he could not be expected to contradict his own sex. In Eve he set woman free and made her as a personality in some respects superior to men. It is now up to woman to live up to her ancestress. The Devil can not do more. The same reason explains why there are no female devils. The Devil does not so much distrust the reliability of she-devils as he wishes to reserve to his own sex the privilege of being a Devil. This may be a prejudice—and the Devil is certainly not without prejudices—but it is a fact. Therefore, we can speak only metaphorically of a Devil in woman's shape. What really exists are Devils who, for a certain purpose, don the appearance of a woman. It must, however, be a decidedly unpleasant or abhorrent thought even to a follower of Satan to have carnal intercourse with a Devil in woman's form, as we understand in Marlowe's *Doctor Faustus.* When, on Faust's expressed wish to have a wife, Mephistopheles produces a "devil dressed like a woman," Faust seems to lose all interest in his former desire. The witches, on the other hand, are far better off, for they may have Devils as their lovers—a subject on which we possess a rich amount of authentic testimony.

According to the stand one takes in what must be considered a controversial and hopelessly complicated matter, one might feel that the Devil has still a long way to go if he wants to pay his debt to Eve, or inversely that women had better try to ingratiate themselves still more to the Devil if they want to be helped in their struggle. For the great question is this: Does Eve owe more to Lucifer or is Lucifer more deeply indebted to Eve?

The question forever will remain without a conclusive answer. It is, however, the unanswerable questions that in the spiritual and intellectual history of mankind have proved to be not only the most harassing but also the most productive. Weighty arguments can be adduced for the theory that the balance-sheet favors Eve. It all depends, of course, on the interpretation of the Fall. The Old Testament, taking no cognizance of the natural drives of man, seems inadequate for any interpretation connecting the fall with the sex act. In trespassing God's command, Eve did not fall a victim to an act of temptation or corruption by Lucifer, nor was she motivated by simple curiosity. It needed the promise that she would become like God and know Good and Evil to induce her to make the fatal decision. This idea suggests that the author of the story wanted to picture the moment when man, no longer satisfied with a vegetative life, asked himself the question of existence and its meaning. If this assumption is accepted, the Biblical story would parallel the state of wonder in the face of all that exists which the Greeks considered the beginning of philosophical thought. The great moment of awakening which the Greek genius, with its secular and speculative endowment, characterized as one of intellectual wonder appeared to the old Hebrews, who combined the religious outlook with its practical applications, as a moral decision touching the divine.

As long as we recognize Adam and Eve as our ancestors, we cannot possibly exaggerate the importance of what they did and experienced. Lucifer's promise, divested of its apparent ethical character, reveals an ontological significance. It points to another world beyond that of Paradise, a world the knowledge of which cannot be obtained without risk. One can imagine how the sudden opening of an outlook upon another reality must have shaken Eve's whole being. She became aware of a world ruled by a pair of opposites, wonderfully alive as compared to the eternal passivity of Paradise—a passivity that, seen against the new horizon, had to appear monotonous. The world that Lucifer spread before Eve is the same world he unfolded with less success before the eyes of Christ when he tempted Him with its rule. This world is not the Devil's but man's. It is a world in which man is free to act, and in which every decision is a risk. The instant when Eve visualized this world, Paradise lost its reality and became a myth called the expulsion from Paradise. However, the discovery of the world of men had been preceded by another experience no less important. The serpent had lived in Paradise together with the other animal inhabitants without revealing its true nature. Suddenly it revealed its true nature to Eve. There was now the overwhelming fact that something could be other than it appeared—a traumatic experience. Paradise was shaken to its foundation. From that time on, we all have had to learn from early childhood that things are not what they seem to be and that there is a painful distinction between the world of appearance and the world of reality.

The Bible is not sentimental, nor is it concerned with descriptive or analytical psychology. It relates facts and leaves it to the reader to supply the inner reactions of the actors. Thus we do not know whether the serpent had to make great efforts to persuade Eve or whether Eve found it difficult to seduce Adam. What we do know is that the weight of the situation remained with Eve and that Adam stayed in the background, living a second class existence. It was Eve who was approached by Lucifer; it was she who made the decision and who saw real life opening up before her eyes. Adam had no immediate contact with the new reality. He did not meet Lucifer. Temptation came to him not through Lucifer but through Eve, and he surrendered obediently to her suggestion. In a situation which decided the fate of man, he made no stand of his own. It seems that the unfathomable substance and significance of the biblical story points also to woman's fundamental attitude toward reality which is that of emotional and intuitive immediacy. Adam's role was secondary, he had to form his opinion on what Eve reported. Thus the male mind lives in concepts and it is through concepts that he struggles to arrive at immediacy, while the woman's effort is directed to translating her innate and intuitive insights into conceptual thoughts. It is by no means far-fetched and artificial to extend the biblical story psychologically. The magic gift and genius of the Bible, verifying its characters by means of a scanty narrative of their surroundings and deeds and of a few words uttered, applies fully to the story of the Fall.

Since Eve opened the door, woman's relation to Evil and the Devil is direct and does not require any logical decision on her part. But man's contact with Evil and the

Devil is indirect and requires premeditation and resolution. King Richard III's "I am determined to prove a villain" is truly a man's attitude and cannot be matched in literature even by such great women villains as Kriemhild of the Edda or Lady Macbeth. For the same reason, we do not hear in medieval times of women concluding pacts with the Devil, though cases of their connivance with the Devil abound. The pact as the expression of a formal and logical resolution is the product of a mind that approaches and seizes its object by means of conceptual thought. The typical woman turns to Evil less out of mature consideration than as a result of an inner process that may or may not be conscious. More easily than man she inadvertently glides into Evil. Remorse may occur not as frequently as in man, but if it does, it may be more radical. This is perhaps because the satisfaction of inflicting Evil and the sadistic pleasure of imposing suffering are more developed in most women than in most men.

It is, of course, futile to speculate whether men or women constitute the higher quota of evildoers. Although the situation is changing today, the positions assigned to women in life have at all times been so different from men's that any sound comparison would have to start from an analysis and evaluation of the nature of differences and their effects, a task without end. Under these circumstances, it may be wise to assume that there is no intrinsic difference in the dissemination of Evil among the sexes, and that what there is relates only to the forms of Evil preferred and the reactions of the evildoers to the Evil inflicted.

YAMA-DEATH-DEVIL, Bull Copulating with Woman, 17th-18th century,
Tibetan Buddhist

XVII

THE REALITY OF THE DEVIL

1

We now return to our original problem: Is the Devil a reality? It may seem strange, even paradoxical, to ask this question at this point. But how can we know what a thing is without being certain of its existence? And how can we know whether or not a thing exists if we do not know what it is?

Before entering into these dialectical considerations, we must remember that man from his inception has expended the major part of his mental energies on the products of his erroneous thinking or the figments of his imagination. However, if we abstracted from our history all the ill-founded speculations on the supernatural and its bearing on the ideas of man and the world and the dreams man entertains about the nature and purpose of life and the universe, we would eliminate the sources of inspiration that have contributed most to the formation of the mind. Even disregarding the elements of truth contained in these speculations, we must remember that their very errors and uncertainties have spurred the mind on its adventurous way.

Man has never lived in one and the same objective world, but in many different conceptions of the world created by varying frames of his mind, his intuitions, and his emotional and intellectual interpretations. As we part from the comparatively limited sector of the

perceptible world that constitutes our physical surroundings and consider it, as we must, as a component of
our real, or inner, world, the meaning of reality and of
the real world lose this unambiguous character. World
pictures, world experiences, and world conceptions substitute themselves for the "one" world and its supposedly
uniform reflection in the mind. This applies to the whole
as well as to the parts, since they are integral to the
whole. It applies to the concept of God.

For two thousand years the idea of God has been the
central concept of Western civilization. In spite of this,
the existence of God never has been unconditionally
secured, nor has His essence been shielded from diver-
gent interpretations. We see that in the inexhaustible
apologetic literature dedicated to proving God's existence and to defending Him against doubt and attack.
The vehemence and scope of this effort suggest that the
authors of the apologetic writings, among them the most
illustrious theologians and scholars of the Church, were
not exclusively concerned with the propagation of the
faith and its defense, but that in refuting counterargu-
ments and silencing opposition, they wished to eradicate
their own doubts. In all this, the difficulty, if not the
impossibility, of conferring the sanction of reason upon
a reality deriving its legitimacy from faith becomes
apparent.

The same problem exists in attempting to prove the
existence of the Devil. Though the nature of God and the
Devil be incomparable, the two have this in common:
their reality is fundamentally a matter of faith and of
individual experience beyond logical inference and dem-
onstration by reason.

But let us examine the problem of reality more closely.
How do we usually determine reality and how do our
ways refer to our problem? The first way, that of observation, is obviously of no avail. God has never been

perceived, and those few who claim to have seen God imply that they had an immediate knowledge of His presence, comparing their experience to an indescribable light associated with the sensation of infinite love. As for the Devil, to have seen him implies the perception of apparitions assumed to be the Devil, apparitions with which communication could be established. Mere whisperings and insinuations of a diabolic character do not imply the perception of the Devil himself. The second way of perceiving reality is that of inference from effects that otherwise defy explanations. This is the argument pursued by the classic cosmological proof of God's existence which maintains that the existence of the world requires the Creator-God as the only possible explanation. Neither science nor philosophy justifies this way of reasoning.

True, if the Almighty God whose idea implies the Creator-God is assumed, the supreme cause of the world's existence has been established. However, such reasoning amounts to nothing more than a hypothetical conclusion, because what has to be proved is contained in the premise. The same objection stands against the attempt to explain the existence of Good and Evil by resorting to God and the Devil.

Another source of reality is the authority of common belief at times founded upon, or replaced by, personal or documentary evidence. It need not be emphasized that in so grave a matter as the one in question, so frail a source cannot be trusted.

Related to these ideas of common belief, yet drastically different, is the theory of the archetypes as it has been accepted by certain schools of psychoanalysis. These archetypal ideas, the number of which is limited, constitute the original patterns of the human mind and thereby the imperishable heritage of mankind. Among the archetypes is the idea of God, and very likely that of the Devil in some form or another. The archetypes emerging in manifold realizations determine the history of the mind. In the life of the individual their formation and claim to domination and their ensuing rivalry may cause the well-known perturbations. Dynamic entities that the archetypes are, they reach consciousness in the individual mind. For this reason, the archetypal ideas of God or the Devil do not permit any conclusion with regard to the reality of God and the Devil.

Finally, a source of reality distantly related to the preceding rests on the conviction that we can be sure only of what we ourselves have created, the creator being an individual or a group of any size. The thing created may be concrete or it may be an idea, a system of thought, a pattern of emotional reactions, a fictitious entity of an artistic or religious nature. The moment it is fully alive it faces us as a reality in its own right capable of dominating or even overpowering and destroying its creator. Geniuses in all fields of art—creators of religions; pioneers in science; superior men who fought for intellectual and moral truth, for social justice, or on the battlefield for their ideas—have succumbed to the tyranny of their own conceptions or paid for them with mental disintegration. Under these circumstances, the question cannot easily be dismissed as to whether, or to what extent, such creations belong in those minds where they are found, or emanate from external forces. In many instances it seems as though these creations were the residues of an intuition of the existence of another realm from which they have been singled out and brought to awareness. To say that they originated in the individual would then be an inadequate explanation for the fact that they took root in a soil which in many cases had to be prepared through strict discipline but in others seemed ready to receive them. Indeed a twofold relationship between the individual mind and the transcendental realm can be distinguished according to whether the mind reaches out to and grasps the constituents of the transcendent realm or whether these constituents descend and take root in the mind ready to receive them.

If this theory of creation is accepted, it follows that all creation is fundamentally re-creation the more perfect it becomes. The creative genius is he who is destined to ascend to the superhuman realm and to bring to man's consciousness some of the illuminations he received, just as Prometheus did not himself invent the fire but removed it from the gods to bestow it on mortal men. Seen from the metaphysical point of view, the achievement of the genius appears not as creation but as re-creation. This, however, in no way reflects upon his merits. On the human plane, he remains sovereign, and the spontaneity of his creativeness continues unimpaired. Any original re-creation bears the distinctive mark of its human re-creator. But this theory of creation, plausible as it may seem, is not demonstrable, and therefore no reality can be inferred with certainty.

As for religion, the believer who models himself after the idea he holds of the divine—or, for that matter, of the diabolic—considers his transformation proof of the reality of his belief; but such proof does not necessarily convince others. To the academic question of whether it is possible to arrive at the conviction of the reality of the divine by the attempt to create or re-create it in oneself, the skeptic has the ready answer: every believer, provided his faith be not simply naïve or conventional, makes use of this method as a result, and at the same time as a guarantee, of his belief without being aware of it.

Considerations of this kind may have led to the contemporary phenomenon of investigations into extrasensory experiences and to the pursuit of abnormal phenomena that the Middle Ages ascribed to the influence of the Devil; particularly apparitions—accoustical and visual phenomena and hypnotic trances induced through the use of hallucinogenic drugs. This laborious and dangerous technique centers on the intentional and systematic production of accoustical and visual hallucinations. It has been proved that it is possible to become evil for scientific purposes without having evil motives. It also is true that one can become a prey of the Devil without believing in his existence. The struggle between the normal self and the imagined divine personality is the same. For it is a struggle between the phenomenon itself and the transcending of the phenomenon. There, too, at the end of the struggle, the normal self may retain the power to withdraw or it may hand itself over to the divine and disappear in God in whatever form He may have been conceived. Nor is the possibility of insanity less likely. The fake saint, or the God-inspired and God-possessed, deceiving himself and others, is a phenomenon known in all creeds. It is evident that by all such techniques and methods nothing can be achieved, and the problem of the reality of God and the Devil remains unsolved.

2

Since there is no way of demonstrating beyond doubt the reality of God and the Devil, and since individual experience cannot claim universal recognition, another approach to the problem must be found—an approach which, though it does not offer a solution, may contribute to its clarification. This approach concerns God's and the Devil's *relation* to reality. Although it is not possible to determine the reality of God and the Devil, it can be demonstrated that God and the Devil differ in their relation to reality. It is implied in the essence of God that

His title to reality is unconditional; He is the absolute being. But the Devil's claim to reality is less pretentious. To be sure, the Devil's virtues always must be taken *cum grano salis* (with a grain of salt).

God demands that His existence be unconditionally recognized. He even insists that there cannot be any doubt with regard to His nature insofar as it can and should be known to men. True, there is the *deus absconditus*, the hidden God, accessible if at all only to the select few; but this is not the God of our world. Yet, if there is no doubt that God wants His existence recognized, it is all the more difficult to understand why this demand is not universally fulfilled. Even when and where the demand is fulfilled, it is rarely accompanied by the full implication of God's meaning. The only explanation is that the belief in God's existence is itself a meritorious act. This idea is sufficient reason why the impossibility of proving God's existence to the intellect in an irrefutable way coexists with His wish to see it recognized.

Strange as it may seem, the Devil's interest in having his existence recognized is considerably less. To begin with, there is general agreement that it is much easier to believe in the existence of God than in that of the Devil. What prompts men to deny or question God's existence is usually some argument based on reason, such as the inadequacy of the proofs adduced, incompatibility with scientific thinking, the impossibility of explaining the coexistence of Evil, etc. Compared to the weight of these weapons, emotional motives such as human pride and presumption are of minor importance. In the case of the Devil, the reverse is true. Reason alone cannot raise more valid objections against the existence of personified Evil than against personified Good. It is our feeling that rebels against the personification of Evil has its terror, although personified Evil, as we stated earlier, is less uncanny than the impersonal power of Evil. In any case, measured by the little emotional resistance that may oppose the belief in God, that which opposes the existence of the Devil is incomparably more vehement.

To the greater difficulty of believing in the existence of the Devil corresponds the lesser interest of the Devil himself in having his existence recognized. God deals straightforwardly with men. He reveals himself as far as it is for the benefit of men and He expects corresponding sincerity and devotion. Were God to reveal himself in the fullness of His splendor, many would despair under the crushing realization of the distance that separates them from God; nevertheless, nobody would turn away from God. If the Devil appeared in his real shape and greatness, quite a few might be magically attracted to him and become his victims; but the majority would turn away horror-struck. What is true of the knowledge of God's and the Devil's nature applies equally to the knowledge of their existence: the belief in the existence of God alone is not sufficient to make us good, but it is a support to which we can have recourse at any time. On the other hand, the firm belief in the existence of the Devil would produce a deterrent influence just as strong as the knowledge of his true nature. So it is in harmony with God's nature and intentions to reveal His existence to those who might want to believe, and it is in the interest of the Devil to remain a speculation.

How subtle is the Devil's strategy. To urge unconditional recognition of his existence would in his case be just as shortsighted as it would be a mistake to have his existence denied. Insecurity against the background of possibility or probability serves his purpose best. In this way he attracts the lukewarm, seduces the hesitating and perplexed, stirs curiosity, temptation, and audacity, and acts as the great challenge to the hero and the saint. This is why, unlike God, the Devil does not insist on his reality. It is, rather, God who wants us to believe in the Devil and who cautions us against him so that we seek refuge with God. The Devil himself does not want us to believe in him; satisfied with speculation, he waits for the moment when the desire of the candidate for hell makes it profitable to substitute appearance for assumption or belief. If this tactic is artful, yet it is sound and unpretentious and may in this respect compare favorably with God's way which demands unconditional belief but withholds experience.

If we regret that neither a flat affirmation or denial of the Devil's existence is possible, we misconstrue the problem. We have seen that if the Devil exists he must appear in a speculative form. This is the face that he must turn to us, so this must be his reality for us. There is no way but to acquiesce in this knowledge.

A metaphysician might elucidate the delicate problem still more and speak in favor of the Devil's reality: the Devil is not, like God and the angels, an unambiguous being. As a result of the fall, he lost his unequivocal determination. Before, he was denizen of the realm of unconditioned existence. In severing the tie which bound him to that realm, he denied his essence and, in a certain sense, compared with what he had been before, became a conditioned existence. Seen from the angle of metaphysics, he now stands between being and not being. So what has been called his suspended reality cannot simply be identified with uncertainty, and his existence characterized as questionable. The uncertainty must be seen and understood against the metaphysical background. If so, the uncertainty loses its seemingly negative meaning; indeed, it reflects the essence of the Devil that situates him between being and not being because he participates in both. What appears as suspended existence, then, would conceal the formidable secret of the Devil's fate and at the same time constitute the very guarantee of his existence.

Having arrived at this conclusion, one cannot help thinking of man. Man also has lived his fall, and though it cannot compare with the Devil's, it was fateful enough because it changed the whole being of man. Ever since, the question whether man really *is*, or can reach, the plane of being or simply a transient phenomenon without substance has not been silenced. If we ponder this relationship with the Devil, we cannot help realizing that in dealing with the Devil's reality we consider our own station and the problem of our reality—with this difference, it is true, that we are the masters of our fate and that it is up to us to decide between being and not being. For if such decision were not within our power, neither God nor the Devil would take so deep an interest in so frail a creature as man.

There is no need—if it is at all possible—to investigate the forms the turn to being may assume or to ask the question by what sign it can be known that the turn has been made. Such questions are difficult to answer, since the turn must not be the outcome of a conscious decision. More often this seems to happen below the threshold of deliberation and intention, and it expresses itself in action or emotion, the significance of which only later will come into the open. Even *homo religioso*, the religious type of man, rarely makes an explicit resolution that leads to a clear result. That is why the well-known documentation of Pascal's mystic experience of November 23, 1654, is unique. True, the experience does not contain the decision itself, but it is the culmination, consecration, and reward of the decision, and therefore at least can compete with the latter in importance. What in the line of our argument is so significant is the repeated exclamation, "Joy, joy" in the sense of beatitude. In the shocklike experience, the violent commotion, and the intuitive insight of the experience, this word unmistakably stands out as the emotional acme describing the atmosphere of the turn to God.

The heretical question must be asked: Is there also on the side of Evil such illumination, ecstasy, and happiness? To answer this question we must forget about the bugbear Devil and similar products of popular medieval imagination. We must dismiss even the idea that the Devil is but the insidious and contemptible enemy of God and that he is Evil only because of his revolt and enmity against God. We must read it, rather, the other way. At the risk of contradicting the Christian view, we must assume that there is Evil in its own right, or at least that Lucifer by his fall created Evil as an autonomous principle, a principle that is not based exclusively on the opposition to God. Then only may we free ourselves from all petty ideas of the nature of the Devil and face him as he is, a great lord in his own sphere.

As God's image is little with the little and great with the great, so it is with the Devil's. Once we understand this, it becomes clear that the conversion to Evil can be as great an act as the conversion to saintliness and the Good. It is a nursery tale that the Devil has nothing in store for his converts but torture and remorse. They feel satisfaction and happiness, illumination and consummation, no less than do the saints of God. Acceptance of this view does away with the all-too-narrow conception of Evil as being nothing but the negation of and opposition to the saintly and the Good. It also eliminates the conception of Evil as being but the punishment for the violation of the saintly and the Good. But no matter. Restoring Evil's original and independent greatness also enhances the glory of the saintly and the Good, and thereby confers greater dignity upon the world of men.

Fra Angelico (1387-1455), *THE LAST JUDGEMENT*

XVIII

THE CHOICE

There is no denying that religious indifference* in the West, and perhaps all over the world, is steadily increasing. In the West this is the result of militant atheism that, around the middle of the eighteenth century, turned against the idea of a personal God as it is taught by the monotheistic creeds. But indifference is the enemy religion must fight, for militant atheism emphasizes and challenges the adversary whereas indifference ignores it or opportunistically dons the disguise of faith or orthodoxy.

It is not too much to say that in our time indifference has in a certain way succeeded in transforming the spirit of conversion. The motives of conversion today are despair, the impossibility of finding one's way in life, the lack of support and consolation, an inner void—ills for the cure of which man turns to religion as the last resort. The ardent desire to believe, the passionate love that on earth finds no adequate object, the deep feeling of security that relies on God as its guarantee—such positive incentives to faith are no longer ours. These incentives may be connected with the experience of the presence of God, of the greatness of the human soul, of the order of the universe. However, the scientific mind discounts these time-honored fundamentals of faith.

Psychology, if it recognizes at all the existence of a

soul—substance, directs its introspection to other phenomena and in another spirit than does religion. And
modern physics, by ever widening the gap separating the
world of sense perception from the world of physics—a
gap in which Newton's world picture still permitted the
union of the visible world and the one revealed by
science in the experience of a God-created universe—
exacts from the natural mind and its will to believe an
effort that makes it ever more difficult to understand
and to experience the universe of modern physics as the
great God-created order. The atomic structure of the new
world picture is less immediately convincing than the
order of the visible world and that of the Newtonian
world picture. The substitution for the sense-perceived
world of a reality so radically different appeals to the
scientific mind and stirs intellectual amazement and
admiration, but it can hardly hope to awaken the deep
emotion with which Newton himself not only affirmed
but strengthened the belief in God and a divine order. On
the contrary, a world picture that increasingly excludes
experience and intuition and in which empty space
seems more of a constituent of matter than matter itself
(that is, the infinitesimal particles themselves of which
new kinds may at any time be discovered)—such a world
picture may convince the physicist of the greatness of
the world and its creator; but in the layman it arouses
feelings of helpless stupor, infinite destitution, and loneliness.

The idea man has of himself must change. He may well
congratulate himself upon the achievements of science
and the gifts he continually receives from its application;
but the knowledge that all this comes from a world in
which he is a stranger, a world that has little to do with
the eternal problems facing him, must finally dispirit
him and weaken the core of his life. The scientist may be
able to shun the dilemma and its consequences, but it is

difficult to see how his fellow man can keep pace with a process that involuntarily seems to threaten his central being.

The rapidly evolving science-determined world is inspired by the idea of creating a better life for all men. Its philosophy of humanitarian relationalism, as we may call it, is allergic to opposition. It is not hostile to religion, but it does not want to be disturbed by dogma. Its domineering categories are true and false, preferably in the form of exact and inaccurate. Correspondingly, in the realm of will, the Good and the bad often assume the meaning of expedient and harmful and the saintly and the Evil hover unobtrusively at the periphery. Another misplaced pair of opposites is that of deep and shallow.

It is, of course, the spirit of science that is ill-disposed— and rightly so from its own viewpoint—to these categories. The deep, and for that matter the shallow, have their own jurisdiction. A thought, a system of thought, an emotional experience, or a work of art may be deep; but they must be neither true nor false, Good nor bad, saintly nor Evil. Even if these pairs of opposites, particularly the two last ones, are applicable to the deep—shallow category, their application is secondary and does not impair its validity. The deep cannot be reduced to the true, the saintly (sacred), nor the Good; nor the shallow to the false, the Evil, nor the bad. There is a natural relationship between the deep and its correspondences, such as the true, as between the shallow and its correspondences, such as the false. However, the Evil or the false may become deep, and the true or the Good shallow, thus establishing the independence and in a certain way the preeminence of the deep-shallow opposition.

Deep and shallow, then, are sovereign in a realm of their own, just as are true and false, sacred and Evil, Good and bad. And the deep and the shallow in the history of mankind play at least as important a role as the other pairs of opposites, as can be seen in the myths and sagas of the great Eastern peoples or of our Middle Ages. The question "true or false?" applied to all of these creations is not only inadequate but falls into empty space. They must be understood and appreciated as transcending the "true and false" category as well as that of the real and unreal. They claim to be deep, that is, to throw light on regions that are inaccessible to daily thought and experience. Proof is that they are interpreted ever anew, not because they are deficient or unclear but because they are deep, a quality that has nothing to do with obscurity.

This also holds for the original system of philosophy beginning in the West with the pre-Socratic philosophers. They expressed their visions in forms that have been paradigmatic to their followers for more than two thousand years. Was what they had to say true? The question is neither justified nor adequate because it fails to recognize the nature of their insights, which is depth. As lightning illuminates darkness, they illuminated being and nonbeing, our own essence and the way we are placed in the universe and cope with its riddles. So it is with all great systems or intuitions of philosophy, Western or Eastern. They rend the darkness around and within us and they do so not because they are true but because they are deep.

This also is true of great works of art which inspire us and permit us to see into the depth of things. The deep is not necessarily true, but it can never be false. Indeed, there is something beyond and above the true from which the changing truths may draw inspiration and strength. A period that lives under the sign of the deep differs in attitude, weight, and evaluation from one that is indifferent to depth.

This detour was necessary in order to arrive at a fair

appreciation of our time. Our time is penetrating, but it is not deep. We sincerely want to get to the roots of phenomena, but we want to do it quickly because we want to make full use of the knowledge. So the phenomena must be classified, the methods of approach determined, the results evaluated. This is not the atmosphere in which depth thrives. Physics and psychology penetrate with ever-growing perspicacity into their worlds. But depth in these fields leads ever further away from the data of immediate experience.

On the other hand, genuine depth as a category precedes experience in the form of a metaphysical conception of the philosophical mind or the transcendent vision of the great artist. The creation of the genius is great not because it is right and true but because it is deep. Future evolution may prove it not true or not altogether right, but such objection will not impair its depth or its effect. As for religion, the scientific interest in religion and religious phenomena in our time is superior to the power of belief and experience. The nineteenth and twentieth centuries have produced an astounding literature on the origin of religion, its evolution and species, on the varieties of religious experience, the relation of religion to psychiatry, etc. But the very disposition and attitude that make this effort possible blocks the way to strong and all-embracing faith and experience such as were the prerogative of other periods. Again, these are penetrating investigations, but by their very nature they move in another atmosphere than that of the deep.

With the weakening of the belief in God, the belief in the Devil seems to have suffered. There is, however, no strict interdependence. The Devil hardly needs religious belief to exert his power. Still less does he require the mood of agnosticism and skepticism, for he who doubts will question the Devil's existence too. What the Devil requires is a general capacity and will to believe. This requirement Western civilization has amply satisfied since the decline of religious faith in the second half of the eighteenth century when belief in the omnipotence of reason inherited the throne of religion. To what extent reason had misunderstood itself as well as religion soon became obvious. During the French Revolution, reason, arrogating to itself the control of minds and an infallibility worthy of religion, produced pseudo-theorems that posed as self-evident truth but in reality were conditioned by the trends and requirements of the time and shared with them their uncertainty and ambiguity. This is conspicuous in Rousseau's theory of the general will as the source and expression of the sovereignty of the people. In the name of the general will, such interpreters and prophets of the new doctrine as Saint-Just and Robespierre silently submitted to the guillotine, that most conspicuous instrument of the people. A similar fate has befallen many Russians in the Communist Revolution, which not only destroys its adversaries in the name of the general will and of humanity but, like the French Revolution, finds its victims among the liberators themselves and condemns them in the name of the purity of the revolution and for the purpose of safeguarding the state.

We see the same pattern in Fascism and National Socialism. Both systems are irrational in essence. Fascism did not even care to develop an explicit and officially recognized theory, but the claim to express the will of the people connects Fascism and National Socialsim with their rationalistic predecessors and opponents. One might easily assume that the record of murder and persecution, of moral and intellectual perversion, that distinguishes at least three of these movements (Fascism as a whole being less steeped in such infamies) would deeply satisfy the Devil. But such an assumption would ignore the implications of these facts and the true nature of the Devil. There is indeed reason to believe that, as a result of the appearance on the political scene of the masses, meanness and the ensuing misdeeds have grown in geometric proportion. However, it is doubtful that modern moral and criminal pathology is so much different from the pathology of previous aristocratic and ecclesiastic powers. Righteousness, a belief in individual rights, and the lust for power are common to both eras. No, the danger of our days is that mass standards steadily infuse our lives. And this danger, which culminates in the bias to foster and serve what is believed to be the will of the majority, is insufficiently balanced by the increasing effort to educate the people because the aims and methods of education are ever more inclined to bow and adjust to those mass standards. We might even venture to say that a mass mind is developing in history.

The Devil is a fanatic individualist. He hates and despises anything that smells of mass and mass spirit. He therefore has nothing directly to do with the modern masses. But he fishes in troubled waters and profits by the confusion connected with mass movements, particularly at their start. Confusion is a state of mind that causes fear and anxiety, and while mass movement is ready to redeem man at the price of his personality and free will, man may still look for help from God or the Devil. The deterioration of political and intellectual life must be attributed to the mass leaders, not to the Devil. This applies particularly to the modern dictators and their underlings, who shape ideas and methods in such a way that they can easily be swallowed and absorbed by the masses. The end is the depersonalization of the people, their disintegration into one homogeneous mass, a soulless tool.

Such techniques may seem diabolical, but we must beware of hasty conclusions. The Devil accepts us no more easily than God does. Indeed, perhaps he accepts us less easily, since he has nothing equivalent to God's mercy. It is impossible to generalize, but perhaps good faith, self-deception, lack of insight, the influence of others, the thirst for revenue, an abnormally developed lust for power and cruelty, and monomaniac ideas such as persecution mania are strong enough to rescue the monster from hell, and this perhaps against his own ambition and desire. The optimistic idea of man as an originally and naturally good and wise creature, which is at the bottom of Rousseau's philosophy, inspired and accompanied Socialism all along its way with the exception of some representatives of Russian revolutionary socialism—anarchism—who indulged in a pessimistic or, rather, a tragic conception of man. However, it has taken modern dictatorship to transform the optimistic view of human nature into one of radical pessimism and to make man a contemptible being. Indeed, what could a ruler think of a creature who welcomes indoctrination with a monomaniac idea, mechanical regulation, of its material and mental life and accepts existence under a police state? Was not Mussolini fundamentally right when he showed the absurdity of Rousseau's theory of the infallibility of the common will in declaring that even if he stood alone with his opinion he still would voice the true Italy?

In any case, modern mass dictatorship is at least as much a product of the masses, as the masses owe their mass character to dictatorship. Under these circumstances it is difficult to pass on the modern dictators a supreme sentence of condemnation that would hand them over to the Devil. Of all of them, Hitler would stand the best chance of being received into the infernal kingdom. The boundlessness of his lust for power without any constructive idea behind it; the indifference to the nature of the means to serve his purpose; his reckless egocentricity revealed in his sexual apathy and in his incapacity for any deep human relationship—all this indicates that men and things were to him but pawns. More characteristic, perhaps, was the enjoyment of his power and the way he gloated over his enemies' defeats and sufferings; he never tired of seeing the film, made on his order, of the deliberately protracted agony of the men who had directly or indirectly participated in the attempt on his life.

For the loss he suffers from the extension of the mass mind and the obliteration of personality, the Devil finds compensation in selected specimens of mass leaders. Although many of them may be made of the same material as the masses, they rise above the masses by the deliberate use they make of them. In any case, it is for the sake of the leaders alone that the Devil takes a positive interest in mass movements. God, too, is averse to the mass phenomena. But he looks at the individual men composing the mass with commiseration, never losing the hope that they will discover their own selves. The Devil takes peremptory stand, for his idea of personality differs in a vital point from that of God's. God maintains man within his natural ties—the family and social group and in the self-created loyalties such as those arising from profession and citizenship—because these ties are the conditions of development and self-realization. Not so the Devil. Fanatic individualist that he is, he denies that the individual can and should be divided among such spheres of existence. Disregarding their positive character, he tries to separate man from his bonds so that man in isolation finds himself in the presence of the Devil, the lonely one standing face to face with the lonely one.

God does not isolate man, and man, the social animal, grows his bonds from the tiny family circle to the world community. To the Devil this is an abomination. He mercilessly unmasks all these unifying devices as artificial efforts to bridge the chasm that separates man from man. To him, all sentiments and emotions that seek to reach another person to draw him near to us in friendship or love are self-deception, an instinctive thirst for breaking the prison wall, but one that never will be quelled. The multitudes, of course, remain ignorant of their situation. Some who feel that they are walking on treacherous ground seek refuge with God. But those who knowingly have looked into the unreality and vanity of all human ties turn to the Devil. They understand that he lives up to what he knows to be true. He alone discloses mercilessly a merciless truth because he lives it, and so he takes their fate to heart. We are probably not too far from reality if we think of hell as the abode of those who are fully conscious of their transcendent loneliness. Needless to say, they are not the only inhabitants of hell, not even the most numerous, but what is certain is that they belong to hell's aristocracy.

It would be a gross error to look at this argument as mere speculation. Although it claims wider significance, it also points to one of the main trends of our time: the move toward the uprooting of natural ties and all traditional order. This trend is the steady expansion of the mass mind. Whether the dissolving of natural ties and the traditional order are interpreted as the condition of this expansion, as one of its components or as the result, so much is certain: the mass mind inadvertently creeps into judgment and reactions. Those who prove invulnerable pay for their resistance with isolation.

What we call mechanization of our lives is the fact that for all situations in our material and mental life— and the number and varieties of these situations are determined and foreseen—the visible or intellectual tools are at hand and have only to be applied to work out the problem. This would seem a perfect world if boredom did not sometimes darken the horizon—not fiercely or militantly but unobtrusively and unpretentiously. Boredom has a subtle and insidious way of hollowing and undermining vitality and, in the end, the will to live. The rapidly changing background and scenery of our daily life, beginning with the political scene and ending with the incessant stream of news, sensations, pleasures, and gadgets, is not the result of boredom but, to some extent, its cause. The continuous flux of changing impressions makes it ever more difficult to concentrate on things and to live with them, and this incapability, together with what might be called surface-consciousness, demands ever-new nourishment and thus closes a vicious circle. Those who fall victims to this process feed on the goods that continuously flow from the assembly line.

Boredom, though it may never come to the foreground, may still work in the dark. Apparent freedom from it may simply indicate under the given circumstances that the mechanization of man has fully triumphed. Yet boredom may still grow in concealment and one day become a serious disease of the social body and explode under various disguises. People, although well fed and clad, may come forward with all kinds of claims and demands for the simple reason that they cannot stand boredom any more.

Seen from the psychological or, to be more precise, spiritual aspect, boredom is the lowest, the least dignified, and emptiest form of loneliness. It is negative loneliness. It feeds indifferently on changing contents of which it consumes infinite quantities because there is no qualified ego-substance to select and assimilate the material. That is why boredom is so widespread and so dangerous.

Positive loneliness, on the other hand, runs through various types and stages to the great loneliness which we characterized earlier. There is the type that shows a

serious and selective interest in objects but is incapable
of putting this interest to any theoretical or practical
use; another deals efficiently with the objects but lacks
emotional reaction; a third feels that nothing can satisfy
him and turns away in disgust. There are many more
whose description would require the idiom of differen-
tial psychology or literary art. They all suffer from the
failure to bridge the gap separating them from objects
and to live effectively with their outer and inner environment. They feel this failure the deeper because the mass
spirit holds out before their eyes the easy solution they
are unwilling or incapable of accepting. Nor do they
possess the diabolical insight of those who are daring
enough to recognize that it is vain to try to establish a
genuine relation with anything, least of all with one's
fellow men, through knowledge or sentiment.

However, we have not yet touched the bottom of our
present situation. In the last resort, it is not even the
relation to the object that today has become problematic,
although—indeed, *because*—the masses have eliminated
the problem by permitting the object or another's will to
determine their actions and feelings. No. For those who
suffer an uncertain and disturbed relation to the object,
it is in reality the relation to their own ego that is
thrown into confusion. In this predicament, neither
isolation nor companionship helps. Both are contami-
nated from the beginning because they are perceived by
a mind that has lost the genuine relation to itself. For
these (and not only for these) Paul Valéry (*Eupalinos*)
has coined the word of abysmal truth: "Quelle âme
hesiterais a bouleverser l'univers pour être un peu plus
ellemême?" (Which soul would hesitate to overthrow the
universe to be a bit more itself?)

The greatness of the human soul, even more the
significance the soul has for itself, is contained in these
words, and therewith the problem every soul faces: to

come to, and to be, itself. Thus what is questionable is not the visionary clarity and truth of Valéry's statement. What is subject to doubt is whether it is permissible to purchase the experience of being a bit more oneself at the price of overthrowing the universe. The Devil would be the first to affirm and sustain the destructive will, for means as well as aims show truly satanic proportions and greatness. And to the Devil the consolidation of the individual personality is worth any price. This is his incomparable chance in these bewildered days of ours where the saint is forgotten and Evil is forgotten or ill-defined, and where Good and bad merge into each other.

The Devil is deadly serious in his endeavor to save and preserve the individual personality at any cost. Whoever entrusts his fate to him may be confident that he has won the support of a mighty ally who will carry him through all dangers to emerge in full possession of his emptied self. But he must be prepared to pay the price. The Devil is lord of loneliness, thus the price will be loneliness, absolute loneliness. How many are able to bear this fate we do not know, nor do we know whether the end is worth the price.

God has another conception of the human person. To Him, there is no personality not intrinsically connected and bound with a world other than the subject's own. Even the hermit is not alone. There is always God if he wants Him. For God does not know absolute loneliness. To the Devil, the other—person or thing—is but delimitation, nonego, enemy. In the realm of God, the other offers the possibility of enlarging, transcending, and enriching the self despite the danger of being threatened and undermined.

Thus God's and the Devil's ways part. There certainly is greatness on both sides. In our endeavor to hold out against the powers of a time that knowingly or unknowingly ignore or suspiciously look at the autonomous personality, we may with certainty rely on God or on the Devil. The choice is ours.

REFERENCES

The quotations from the HOLY BIBLE are taken from the King James Version (Oxford University Press/British Bible Society) with a few from the Revised Standard Version when noted (RSV).

p.3 Terence, *HEAUTONTIMOROUMENOS*, Act I, Scene I, Line 25.

p.8 Alfred North Whitehead, *PROCESS AND REALITY* (New York: The Macmillan Company, 1929).

p.15 Alfred North Whitehead, *PRINCIPLES OF RELATIVITY* (Cambridge: Cambridge University Press, 1922).

p.57 *MALLEUS MALEFICARUM (THE WITCHES' HAMMER)*, trans. Montague Summers.

p.77 Goethe, *FAUST*, trans. Bayard Taylor (New York: Oxford University Press, 1952)

p.96 Charles Williams, *WITCHCRAFT* (London: Faber & Faber, 1941).

p.187 I refer to the disreguard of a true religious experience. The present convulsive, vulgar, "religious" fanaticism such as the creationist sects in the world reveals the loss of the transcendent and represents the tragedy of this century. It is the irreligious agony of our time. It constitutes a denial of the true Good, of spiritual, moral, and intellectual probity as well as of God whom the "religious" fanatics profess to revere.

INDEX